Study Guide

for use with

Fundamentals of Financial Accounting

Sixth Edition

Daniel G. Short
Glenn A. Welsch
Both of
The University of Texas at Austin

IRWIN
Homewood, IL 60430
Boston, MA 02116

ISBN 0-256-07732-0

2 3 4 5 6 7 8 9 0 V 6 5 4 3 2 1 0

Contents

Study Suggestions for the Student

This Study Guide is a supplement to *Fundamentals of Financial Accounting*. Its purpose is to help you learn those features of financial accounting that are necessary in understanding, interpreting, and using financial information. It is designed to assist you in reviewing the subject matter of the textbook, to self-test your knowledge of each chapter, and to provide some guidance for further study of the materials. This study guide provides the following:

1. A statement of the purpose of each chapter.
2. Suggestions on how to study each chapter.
3. A study outline of each chapter for *review purposes*.
4. A series of questions for *self evaluation* of your knowledge (approximately 500 questions).
5. Answers to the questions for self evaluation.

A logical and realistic study plan consistently followed will assure success in your first course in accounting. Experience has demonstrated to us that the use of this study guide will increase your knowledge without undue expenditure of additional time. The review and self evaluation features increase your level of competence in completing homework and examinations. Accounting is learned best by understanding the concepts, standards, and the reasons why (rationale) of accounting, rather than by memorization. Accounting is similar to mathematics in many ways. That is, accounting is logical; it provides fairly precise answers, and "problems" must be solved to make the learning process effective. Thus, completion of the questions for self evaluation (and the assigned homework) will contribute significantly to the learning process. Also, there is a cumulative feature of accounting. Each chapter constitutes a building block for the chapters that follow. Your success in the later chapters (and later accounting courses) is related to the level of comprehension attained earlier. If you do not master each link (chapter) in sequence, your chances for later success are reduced significantly. If followed consistently, the study suggestions given below will significantly enhance your potential for success in accounting.

Use of the textbook. When you start a chapter, read all of it carefully (or that portion assigned by your instructor). The word "carefully" is used advisedly because an accounting textbook *cannot* be read like most other books. The material discussed is cumulative and is characterized by some complexity. Prior to reading the chapter, the purpose and the sequential captions should be noted with care because they focus on the central issues discussed in the chapter. As you read the chapter, usually it is advisable to make margin notes (often questions) as a reminder that restudy is desirable (or to pose a question in class). Throughout your study of a chapter focus on the logic of the explanations (the concepts) and the reasons why. Be sure to study carefully each example and illustration.

After the first reading, return to certain parts of the chapter for in-depth study. If after sustained effort you do not understand the material, you should be prepared to ask specific and relevant questions in class. The troublesome questions should be cleared up before the next chapter is studied.

Finally, **always be prepared before the class meeting.** If you are behind in studying the chapter, you are apt to gain very little from the class discussions. The farther you fall behind, the more difficult it is to catch up. The chapters should be studied regularly; cramming just before the examinations simply does not work in an accounting course.

Note-taking. We strongly recommend that you take notes on the important items discussed in class. This is a valuable aspect of the learning process and provides review of materials for items emphasized by your professor. In addition, your professor supplements the discussions in the textbook at most class meetings. The supplementation includes new ideas, new examples, extension of discussions in the text, and more significantly, interpretations and logical explanations of the subject matter. Professors naturally tend to emphasize on examinations those issues that they emphasized in the class discussions. Therefore, your note-taking can be quite helpful.

Homework assignments. Homework is assigned by your professor to (a) provide a learning experience; (b) apply concepts, standards, and procedures; (c) learn to do by doing; and (d) test your knowledge and proficiency. It is one thing to understand an explanation in the text (or by your professor), but quite a different matter to apply it in a realistic or problem situation on your own. One cannot learn accounting only by reading descriptions of it, no matter how many times the description is read. As with mathematics, accounting can be learned only by both reading about it and actually *doing it*. This latter phase of the learning process is what happens when your homework involves exercises, problems, and case situations. We cannot overemphasize the importance in learning accounting of completing your homework assignments.

To solve the homework assignments efficiently, and with maximum benefit, we recommend the following steps:

a.   Read the requirements very carefully.
b.   Read the problem carefully and note all relevant facts. Except on very short problems, note the relevant facts on a scratch pad or underscore them in your text.
c.   Relate the facts to the requirements and decide upon a solution approach.
d.   Solve the problem. When necessary refer to the chapter for assistance on specific points. Show computational steps where appropriate. (You may want to use the solution forms given in the separate working papers.)
e.   Review the completed solution. Be sure all of the requirements are satisfied.

When homework assignments are discussed later in class, take notes and make corrections on your solutions. These are valuable for review purposes in preparing for examinations.

Use of this study guide. We believe you can attain maximum benefits from this study guide if you consistently adhere to the following procedures:

a.   Before studying the chapter read the related section in this study guide entitled "How to Study the Chapter."
b.   Complete your reading and study of the chapter.
c.   Complete the homework.
d.   Turn to the section entitled "Study Outline" in this guide for the related chapter. Go over this outline carefully as a review of the chapter. Space is provided throughout the outline for additional notes that you may want to add for future review.
e.   Turn to the section entitled "Questions for Self Evaluation" in this guide for the related chapter. Answer each question and requirement to the best of your ability without referring again to the chapter or to the answers provided in the back of the study guide.
f.   After answering all of the questions to the best of your ability, turn to the solutions in the back of this study guide and grade yourself.
g.   On the basis of your answers, as graded, decide what parts of the chapter you should study further. In respect to those questions on which you were largely unsuccessful, after further study of the chapter, go back and try them again without further reference to the answers.

Preparing for examinations. Examinations are given by your instructor in order to measure your mastery of the subject matter. Examinations often worry students unduly and may lead to considerable nervousness. These understandable conditions usually can be minimized by adequate study on a regular basis and a reasonable review of the major topics. Inadequate preparation causes a lack of confidence which is the real culprit.

The best preparation for examinations, of course, is effective and consistent study of each chapter as it is assigned. The suggestions given above bear on this endeavor. Because a large portion of most examinations in accounting courses involves quantitative problems (i.e., application) that must be solved within a limited amount of time, the ability to work under pressure is important. You can significantly increase your problem-solving (application) competence in accounting by:

a. Working the assigned homework on your own and with some time pressure. You can gain experience in dealing with time pressure by establishing a time budget for each problem.
b. Solving the questions for self evaluation given in this guide with some time pressure. Most of these questions are of the "examination type."
c. Test yourself by reworking selected problems that you have already been exposed to such as completed homework, the study guide questions, and examples given in the chapter (the solution also is there).
d. Read all of the exercises given in the text to be certain that you can solve each one.

Over the years, we have observed that some students waste considerable time while taking an examination. Analyze yourself: Do you waste time sharpening pencils, smoking, erasing, paper shuffling, leaving the room, idleness, etc.?

Our experience also indicates that many students lose "points" because they (a) do not read the "problem facts" carefully (be sure you understand the facts, if not, ask your instructor for clarification) and (b) do not read the requirement carefully (be sure you understand the requirements; if not, ask for clarification).

In taking an examination spend your time on the questions that have the higher weight. If you get "stuck" go on to the next problem. If items are omitted, place a large mark in the side margin so you won't forget to come back to them.

Finally, students often find that working the practice set (published separately as *The Jenelle Group, Inc.* is a useful part of learning the fundamentals of financial accounting.

Perspectives—Accounting Objectives and Communication

PURPOSE OF THIS CHAPTER

In our environment people need information to make rational economic decisions. Most consumers use product and price information prior to purchasing a specific item. Investors and creditors need financial information. Investors and creditors use financial information before they provide funds to a business entity. A primary source of financial information is the periodic financial statements provided by a business entity. The primary purpose of this chapter is to define accounting, review the environment in which accounting is done and to describe how accounting serves our society.

HOW TO STUDY THIS CHAPTER

This chapter focuses on the broad perspectives of the environment in which the accounting function is carried out and accounting communication. You should read it carefully; give particular attention to the broad objectives of accounting in a complex society. The nature of the accounting process and Exhibit 1-2 (in the text) merit your special attention. The Demonstration Case, and the commonsense solution, should be studied; they serve to introduce you to the relevance of accounting at the individual level. You should become familiar with the meaning of the important terms defined at the end of the Summary.

STUDY OUTLINE OF THIS CHAPTER

Part A—The Objectives and Environment of Accounting

A. A society is comprised of a wide range of organizations, such as businesses, governmental units, political groups, churches, professional societies, and social associations. Accounting focuses on the measurement and reporting of financial information in society.

   1. Accounting is an information system designed to **measure, record, and report**, primarily in monetary terms, resources that flow into and out of an enterprise, and the resources (i.e., assets), liabilities, and the interests of the owners.

B. The three primary types of business entities with which accounting deals are:

1. Sole proprietorship—a business owned by one person (the proprietor).
2. Partnership—a business owned by two or more persons as joint owners (the partners).
3. Corporation—a business incorporated under the laws of the state and permitted to issue capital stock as evidence of ownership (the owners are known as stockholders).

C. Measurement fundamentals:

1. Measurement in dollars—the monetary unit (e.g., the dollar) provides the means for expressing the resources and resource flows of an entity.
2. Separate-entity assumption—accounting separates the enterprise from its owners and all other parties for measurement, recording, and reporting purposes.
3. Accounting measures, records, and reports the economic effects of **completed transactions** involving parties external to the enterprise.

D. Accounting serves decision makers (i.e., the financial statement users) in three ways:

1. Provides information which helps them assess the **future** prospects of the enterprise.

2. Provides a continuing measurement of the economic effects of completed transactions of the enterprise.

3. Keeps track of all of the resources (assets) and liabilities, which is a scorekeeping and safeguarding function of the enterprise.

E. Five important groups in the United States currently predominate in the development of financial accounting. They are:

1. Financial Accounting Standards Board (FASB)—an independent board established to develop accounting standards and related guidelines.

2

2. American Institute of Certified Public Accountants (AICPA)—composed primarily of professional accountants in public practice (as opposed to being in the employ of a business).
3. Securities and Exchange Commission (SEC)—a governmental regulatory agency that is responsible for governmental supervision of the sale of capital stock and other securities in interstate commerce.
4. American Accounting Association (AAA)—an association controlled by college accounting professors. It focuses on accounting research and accounting education.
5. Financial Executives Institute (FEI)—a group of financial vice presidents, controllers, and other accounting executives employed in industry.

F. The accounting profession offers many career opportunities. It is represented primarily by the **certified public accountant** (CPA). This designation and its use are controlled by law in a manner similar to that for attorneys and medical doctors. The three broad areas of endeavor by accountants are:

1. Practice of public accounting—involves (a) auditing, (b) management advisory services and (c) tax service. These are rendered as professional services on an independent basis.
2. Employment by organizations—involves serving as a financial officer, controller, chief accountant, analyst, financial planner, etc., as an employee. Accountants employed in these activities often take a professional examination to become a Certified Management Accountant, or CMA.
3. Employment in the public sector—involves serving as a financial officer, chief accountant, analyst, auditor, financial planner for governmental units, etc., as an employee.

Part B—Communication of Accounting Information

G. Communication is a flow of information from one party to one or more other parties. To attain effective communication, the parties must have a common understanding of the information.

1. Accounting communicates to decision makers by means of periodic financial statements. The statements use words (some are technical), numbers, and other symbols.
2. The financial statements are directed primarily to investors and creditors.

H. There are three **required** financial statements specifically designed to communicate to external parties (i.e., owners, creditors, investors, and the public at large). The three required financial statements are:

1. Income statement—reports revenues, expenses, and net income (i.e., profit). See Exhibit 1-4 in the text.
2. Balance sheet—reports assets, liabilities, and owners' equity. See Exhibit 1-5 in the text.

3. Statement of cash flows—reports cash flows from three types of activities: (1) operating activities, (2) investing activities and (3) financing activities. See Exhibit 1–6 in the text.

I. The income statement reports the results of operations for a specific **period of time** such as one year or one month.

$$\text{Revenues} - \text{Expenses} = \text{Net income}$$

   (a) Revenues are earned from the sale of goods or services rendered by the enterprise to others for which the enterprise will receive (or has received) cash or something else of value.

   (b) Expenses are the measure of resources expended or used by the enterprise for which the enterprise will receive (or has received) cash or something else of value.

   (c) Net income is the excess of total revenues over total expenses.
   Net loss is the excess of total expenses over total revenues. Refer to Exhibit 1-4 in the text.

   (d) Earnings per share (EPS) is reported on the income statement and is calculated by dividing income by the number of shares of common stock outstanding.

J. The balance sheet reports the **financial position** of a business at a **given date**. Financial position refers to the amount of resources owned by the business (assets), the amount of debts owed (liabilities), and the claims of the owners (owners' equity). Refer to Exhibit 1-5 in the text.

1. The accounting model for the balance sheet is:

$$\text{Assets} = \text{Liabilities} + \text{Owners' equity}$$
$$\text{or, equivalently Assets} - \text{Liabilities} = \text{Owners' equity}$$

   (a) Assets are resources owned by the enterprise. They may be tangible (physical in character), such as land and buildings, or intangible, such as a patent.

   (b) Liabilities are the debts (obligations) of the enterprise. They arise through the purchase of assets or services from others on credit and through cash borrowings to finance the business.

   (c) Owners' equity is the residual claim of the owners to the assets after deducting the liabilities from the assets. It derives from two sources: (1) contributed capital—the investments by the owners in the business and (2) retained earnings—the accumulated profits of the business less the losses and less all accumulated withdrawals by the owners (i.e., dividends).

4

K. The statement of cash flows (SCF) reports three primary categories of cash flows.

   1. Cash flows from operating activities. These activities are directly related to earning income.
   2. Cash flows from investing activities. This category includes cash flows that are related to the acquisition or sale of productive assets used by the company.
   3. Cash flows from financing activities. These cash flows are directly related to financing the business itself.

1—Questions for Self Evaluation

These questions follow the sequence of the discussions in the chapter. After studying the chapter, try to answer each question to the best of your ability without referring again to the chapter. After answering all of them, turn to the solutions in the back and evaluate yourself. This should provide a valuable guide for deciding how much additional study you should commit to the chapter.

1. An accounting system is designed to: (a) measure, (b) _____ , and (c) _____ in monetary terms the transactions of the entity.

2. The primary purpose of financial statements prepared for investors and creditors is to meet the scorekeeping responsibilities of the enterprise. _____ T; _____ F

3. Accounting records all of, and only, the exchange transactions of the enterprise. _____ T; _____ F

4. The separate-entity assumption is that _____

_____ .

5. Match the following:

Types of Business Entities	*Brief Description*
(1) _____ Corporation	A. A single owner.
(2) _____ Partnership	B. Ownership is evidenced by shares of capital stock.
(3) _____ Sole proprietorship	C. Two or more owners and unincorporated.

6. In a corporation each owner is not responsible for all of the debts of the enterprise. _____ T; _____ F

7. For accounting purposes a sole proprietorship and its owner are separate entities. _____ T; _____ F

8. Complete the following:

Abbreviation	*What the Abbreviation Means*
(1) CPA	_____
(2) GAO	_____
(3) AICPA	_____
(4) FASB	_____
(5) SEC	_____
(6) CMA	_____
(7) AAA	_____
(8) GAAP	_____
(9) FEI	_____

9. The three required financial statements for investors and creditors are:

(1) _____

(2) _____

(3) _____

10. X Corporation reported total expenses of $60,000, and total revenues of $100,000, and an income tax rate of 30 percent. Therefore, net income was:

A. $10,000
B. $70,000
C. $65,000

D. $60,000
E. $40,000
F. None of the above; it was $ _____ .

11. Y Corporation reported total revenues of $150,000, total expenses (including income tax) of $90,000, and 20,000 shares of common stock outstanding. Therefore, EPS was:

A. $7.50
B. $4.50
C. $6.00

D. $3.00
E. $15.00
F. None of the above; it was $ _____ .

12. T Corporation reported: EPS of $2.00, revenues of $90,000 and total expenses of $60,000. Therefore, the number of shares of common stock outstanding was _____ .

13. W Corporation reported total assets of $500,000 and total liabilities of $350,000; therefore, owners' equity was $ _____ .

14. Z Company owned a machine which cost $18,000 when acquired. The machine is used in operating the business and has an estimated useful life to the company of 12 years. Therefore, one year's depreciation expense would be (assuming straight-line depreciation) $ _____ .

15. B Corporation reported pretax income of $30,000 and net income of $24,000; therefore, the income tax rate was _____ % .

16. D Corporation reported total liabilities of $70,000; contributed capital of $100,000, and retained earnings of $25,000. Therefore, the company reported total assets of $ _____ .

17. V Corporation sold 10,000 shares of its $10 par value stock for cash $140,000. Therefore, the "premium" of $ _____ is reported on the balance sheet as _____ .

18. The three types of cash flows reported on the SCF are _____

_____ .

19. The statement that reports the resources owned, obligations owed, and owner's claims is called the

_____ .

20. The statement that reports revenues, expenses, and income (or loss) is called the _____

_____

21. The statement that reports cash flows is called the _____

_____ .

8

22. Brown Company earned revenues of $60,000 and incurred expenses of $51,000. There were five stockholders, and each owned 1,000 shares of the stock of the company.

(a) Net income was: $ _____

(b) Earnings per share was: _____

23. Indicate to the right, with a check mark for each item, the classification on the financial statements.

Item	*Revenue*	*Expense*	*Neither*
(a) Cash balance at the end of the period..................	____	____	____
(b) Sales of goods during the period	____	____	____
(c) Rent incurred (paid) during the period	____	____	____
(d) Utilities (electricity and water)......................	____	____	____
(e) Sales of services during the period	____	____	____
(f) Debts owed at the end of the period for goods bought...	____	____	____
(g) Advertising costs incurred during the period............	____	____	____
(h) Commissions earned by the company during the period	____	____	____
(i) Machinery owned at the end of the period	____	____	____
(j) Interest incurred (paid) during the period	____	____	____
(k) Rent earned during the period	____	____	____
(l) Income tax expenses of the period	____	____	____
(m) Interest earned during the period	____	____	____

24. The purpose of the balance sheet is to report the _____ position of the business on a given date.

25. On a balance sheet, if total stockholders' equity is $75,000 and total liabilities is $25,000, then total assests would be $ _____.

26. (a) Resources owned by the business are called _____.

(b) Obligations owed by the business are called _____.

27. A company owns a machine that cost $12,000 when acquired. To date the accumulated depreciation is $4,000. What is the *net* amount added to assets? $_____

28. In respect to liabilities, an open account owed to a regular supplier usually is called an _____; in contrast, when there is a signed agreement (and usually interest is specified), it is called a _____.

29. The residual interest claim of the owners to the assets (as reported on the balance sheet) is called _____.

30. The two primary sources of owner's equity in a business are: (a) _____ and (b)_____.

9

31. Match each of the following accounting terms with its proper definition by inserting the letter which identifies the definition in the space next to the term.

Accounting Terms

_____ (1) Accounting entity

_____ (2) AAA

_____ (3) AICPA

_____ (4) Assets

_____ (5) Auditing

_____ (6) Balance sheet

_____ (7) Contributed capital

_____ (8) Corporation

_____ (9) Depreciation

_____ (10) Exchange transaction

_____ (11) EPS

_____ (12) Expenses

_____ (13) FASB

_____ (14) GAAP

_____ (15) Income statement

_____ (16) Liabilities

_____ (17) Management advisory services

_____ (18) Net income

_____ (19) Owners' equity

_____ (20) Partnership

_____ (21) Retained earnings

_____ (22) Revenues

_____ (23) SEC

_____ (24) Separate entity assumption

_____ (25) Sole proprietorship

_____ (26) SCF

Definitions

A. Obligations; debts; promise to pay

B. Position statement; assets = liabilities + owner's equity

C. A separate legal entity; shares of stock represents ownership

D. Inflow of resources; from sale of goods and services

E. American Accounting Association

F. Monetary unit used to account for an entity; the dollar; affected by inflation

G. Allocation of cost of operational asset; based on use

H. Attest function; reliability; auditors' opinion

I. A business or other organization; for accounting as a unit

J. An enforceable agreement; resources involved

K. Nonstock; one owner

L. Service rendered by CPS firms; consulting; complements audit and tax services

M. Earnings per share; common stock

N. American Institute of CPA's

O. Financial Accounting Standards Board

P. Business unit; separate from owners; for accounting and reporting purposes

Q. Statement of cash flows

R. Nonstock; two or more owners

S. Required report; operations; income; EPS

T. Total amount invested by stockholders

U. Items owned; have value

V. Revenues – Expenses

W. Securities and Exchange Commission; government

X. Outflow of assets; for goods and services used

Y. Accumulated earnings; reduced by dividends

Z. Generally accepted accounting principles

AA. Assets – Liabilities

The Accounting Model and Transaction Analysis

PURPOSE OF THIS CHAPTER

Chapter 1 emphasized the importance of the communication of accounting information to certain decision makers. It also presented an overview of external financial statements. The purpose of Chapter 2 is to begin our discussions of how the accounting function collects data about business transactions and how that data are processed to provide the periodic financial statements. To accomplish this purpose this chapter discusses the fundamental accounting model; transaction analysis; and how the results of transaction analysis are recorded in an accounting system.

HOW TO STUDY THIS CHAPTER

In this chapter, you will learn how to analyze some simple business transactions in terms of the fundamental accounting model. Also, you will learn how to record the results of transaction analysis in the accounting system. Be sure you understand the material in this chapter before you study subsequent chapters. This chapter provides an important foundation for the rest of this course. If you do not understand this chapter, you will have difficulty with all of the other chapters.

STUDY OUTLINE OF THIS CHAPTER

A.   The Fundamental Accounting Model and Transaction Analysis.

   1.   From Chapter 1, the basic accounting model is:

   Assets (A) = Liabilities (L) + Owners' Equity (OE)

   The accounting model can also be thought of as:

   Resources   =   Sources
      (A)   (L + OE)

   2.   Each transaction has a dual effect in the model. For example, the payment of a debt would decrease both an asset and a liability by the same dollar amount.

   Example: Payment of $2,000 liability.

	Assets	=	Liabilities	+	Owners' Equity
Before	$10,000		$ 2,000		$8,000
Payment	(2,000)		(2,000)		
After	$8,000	=	-0-		$8,000

11

3. After each transaction is recorded, the accounting model is in balance.

4. The basic accounting model can be expanded as follows:

Assets = Liabilities + Owners' Equity

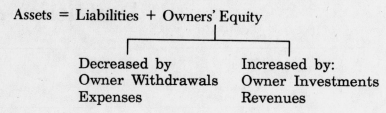

Decreased by	Increased by:
Owner Withdrawals	Owner Investments
Expenses	Revenues

B. Nature of transactions.

1. Accounting focuses on events that have an economic impact on the entity. Transactions include:

    (a) Exchanges between the entity and one or more other entities.
    (b) Other events that do not involve an exchange (e.g., the recording of depreciation expense).

2. Study Exhibit 2-1 in the text. It shows how a number of transactions affect the basic accounting model.

3. Each transaction is analyzed to determine its impact on the accounting model. The transaction is then recorded in terms of its impact on the model.

C. Financial Statement Accounts.

1. A separate account is created for each item reported on the financial statements. An example of a cash account is shown on the following page. These accounts are used to keep track of changes in each item reported on the financial statements.

Left or Debit Side	Cash*		Right or Credit Side	Account No. 101
(Increases)			(Decreases)	
Investment by owners	20,000		To purchase truck	8,000
Loan from bank.....................	5,000		Operating expenses...................	25,800
Cleaning revenue....................	40,000		Interest expense	600
Collections on			Dividends declared and paid	1,800
accounts receivable................	1,000		Payment on accounts payable........	500
	66,000			36,700

*The data shown in this account were taken from Exhibit 2-1 in the text.

2. Accounts facilitate preparation of the financial statements and help attain accuracy in the accounting system.

D. Debits and Credits

1. An account has two sides. The left side is called the debit side and the right side is called the credit side.

2. In recording transactions, the amount recorded as debits must equal the amount recorded as credits.

E. Transaction Analysis—The process of studying a transaction to determine its dual effect on the accounting model.

1. Transactions are recorded under the accrual basis. This means that transactions are recorded when their economic effect occurs and not necessarily when cash is paid or received.

(a) Example: A sale on credit is recorded when the merchandise is delivered to the customer instead of delaying the recording of the sale to when the customer pays the cash that is owed.

2. Journal entry—A method of expressing the results of transaction analysis in a debit/credit format.

   (a) Example: Borrowed $1,000 cash from the bank:

	Debit	Credit
Cash	1,000	
Bank loan		1,000

3. The following shows the effects of journal entries on the accounting model.

Assets		=	Liabilities		+	Owners' Equity	
(Debit)	(Credit)		(Debit)	(Credit)		(Debit)	Credit)
+	−		−	+		−	+

4. Periodic financial statements are prepared from the data accumulated in the accounts (discussed in Chapter 3).

F. Journals and Ledgers

1. Transactions are initially recorded in a journal (i.e. with a journal entry). The journal is a chronological listing of transactions.
2. Ledgers represent all of the individual accounts. In a manual system, the ledger may be a notebook.

G. Chart of Accounts

1. The listing of all of the individual accounts used by a specific business.

2—Questions for Self Evaluation

These questions follow the sequence of the discussions in the chapter. However, they do not cover all of the points discussed in the chapter. After studying the chapter, try to answer each question to the best of your ability without referring again to the chapter. After answering all of them, turn to the solutions in the back and evaluate yourself. This should provide a valuable guide for deciding how much additional study you should commit to the chapter.

1. Most, but not all, exchange transactions involving the enterprise have a dual economic effect in terms of the fundamental accounting model. _____ T; _____ F

2. The forms and other completed papers that underlie or support a transaction usually are called _____ .

3. The fundamental accounting model is:

   _____Assets_____ = _____ + _____

4. Analyze each transaction by entering the appropriate amounts in the tabulation below. Identify each kind of asset (such as cash), liability, and owners' equity affected; indicate increase with a "+" and decrease with a "−" symbol.

Transaction	Assets	=	Liabilities	+	Owners' Equity
(a) Owners invested $5,000 and received 500 shares of capital stock	$		$		$
(b) Purchased machine on credit for use in the business, $2,000					
(c) Service revenue earned, $4,000 of which $3,000 was collected in cash					
(d) Expenses incurred, $2,500 of which $2,000 was paid in cash					
(e) Borrowed $6,000 cash on 15%, one-year, interest-bearing note payable					
(f) Depreciation expense on the machine purchased in (b), $400					
Totals	$		$		$

5. Recording transactions in the journal is usually called _____ .

6. Prepare entries in the journal given below for each of the following transactions completed by Ready Service, Inc.:

(a) January 7, 19A: Collected cash for service revenues, $8,000.
(b) January 12, 19A: Purchased a pickup truck for use in the business, $3,500, paid cash.
(c) January 15, 19A: Borrowed $4,000 cash on 15 percent, one-year, interest-bearing note payable.
(d) January 28, 19A: Completed a service job and billed the customer $6,000; immediately collected $5,000 cash.
(e) January 30, 19A: Paid expenses, $11,000 (cash).

JOURNAL

Page 15

DATE	ACCOUNT TITLES AND EXPLANATION	FO-LIO	DEBIT	CREDIT

7. Analyze the following transactions completed during 19A by CD Service Corporation; then enter them directly in the T-accounts given below. Key the amounts with the letters for identification.

(a) Owners invested $25,000 cash and received 2,500 shares of capital stock (nopar value).
(b) The corporation borrowed $5,000 cash on a 16 percent, one-year, interest-bearing note payable.
(c) Earned service fees of $12,000 of which $11,000 was collected in cash.
(d) Expenses incurred during 19A, $8,000 of which $7,500 was paid immediately in cash.

Cash	Notes Payable	Capital Stock, Nopar

Accounts Receivable	Accounts Payable	Revenues

Expenses

8. The right side of a T-account is called the _____ side and the left side is called the _____ side.

9. There are two "balancing" features of the fundamental accounting model. They are:

(a) _____

(b) _____

10. Provide the appropriate response for each of the following:

(a) Net income increases net assets and also increases_____ .

(b) Resources owned by an enterprise are called _____ .

(c) Goods purchased on credit increases both assets and _____ .

(d) The declaration and payment of a cash dividend decreases assets and also decreases _____ .

(e) Expenses incurred but not yet paid increases _____, and decreases _____ .

17

11. The following journal entries were made by Slich Services, Incorporated:

JOURNAL   Page 8

Jan. 10, 19A	Cash	101	5 0 0 0	
	Revenues	302		5 0 0 0
Jan. 12, 19A	Expenses	404	3 0 0 0	
	Cash	101		3 0 0 0
Jan. 15, 19A	Cash	101	1 0 0 0	
	Accounts receivable	105		1 0 0 0
Jan. 19, 19A	Accounts payable	203	2 0 0 0	
	Cash	101		2 0 0 0

You are to post the above entries to the T-accounts given below.

Cash   No. 101   **Accounts Receivable**   No. 105

Accounts Payable   No. 203   **Revenues**   No. 302

Expenses   No. 404

12. Complete the following matrix by entering either debit or credit in each appropriate cell:

Item	Decreases	Increases
(a) Liabilities		
(b) Assets		
(c) Owners' equity		
(d) Expenses		
(e) Revenues		

13. If debits = credits and assets = liabilities + owners' equity in a trial balance there still can be errors in some of the account balances. _____ T; _____ F

14. A debit to an expense account has the effect of increasing expenses and owners' equity. _____ T; _____ F

15. A machine which cost $15,000 has accumulated depreciation of $9,000 at the end of year 3 since acquisition. Assuming straight-line depreciation and no residual (scrap) value:

    (a) Annual depreciation expense was $ _____.

    (b) The estimated useful life of the machine was _____ years.

16. Match each of the following accounting terms with its proper definition by inserting the letter which identifies the definition in the space next to the term.

Accounting Terms	Definitions
_____ (1) Account	A. The left side of an account
_____ (2) Accrual basis	B. The financial statements that must be prepared each reporting period for external parties (balance sheet, income statement, and statement of cash flows.)
_____ (3) Business (source) document	
_____ (4) Cash basis	C. The right side of an account
_____ (5) Credit	D. An exchange between a business and one or more parties and certain other events, such as a fire loss.
_____ (6) Debit	
_____ (7) Journal entry	E. The process of studying a completed transaction to determine its economic effect on a business in terms of the fundamental accounting model: Assets = Liabilities + Owners' Equity.
_____ (8) Periodic financial statements	
_____ (9) Transaction	
_____ (10) Transaction analysis	F. An accounting method of expressing the results of transaction analysis in a debit-credit format
	G. A document that evidences (supports) a business transaction
	H. The transaction is recorded when the economic effect occurs
	I. The transaction is recorded when cash is paid or received
	J. A standardized format used to accumulate data about each financial statement element.

The Accounting Information Processing Cycle

PURPOSE OF THIS CHAPTER

Chapter 2 emphasized the fundamental accounting model and transaction analysis. It also discussed the use of journal entries and T-accounts to record the results of transaction analysis for each business transaction. The purpose of Chapter 3 is to discuss the accounting information cycle, which processes financial data from the transaction to the end result—the periodic income statement, balance sheet and statement of cash flows. This chapter will expand your knowledge of journal entries, accounts, and financial statements.

HOW TO STUDY THIS CHAPTER

There are many phases (or steps) in the accounting cycle. As you study the chapter, be sure that you understand **why** each phase is necessary and why it occurs when it does. Some students try to memorize the various phases but you should try to understand them.

STUDY OUTLINE OF THIS CHAPTER

A. The accounting information processing cycle is the process of collecting and processing accounting data. It is called a cycle because it must be repeated each accounting period. The phases of the cycle are:

Phases completed throughout each annual accounting period:

1. **Collection of raw economic data**—as each transaction is completed, the source documents are collected and transmitted to the accounting function.

2. **Analysis of transactions**—a mental activity that identifies and measures the economic impact of the transaction in terms of the fundamental accounting model (Assets = Liabilities + Owners' Equity).

3. **Journalizing**—the process of recording in the journal, in chronological order, the results of Phase 2 (for each transaction).

4. **Posting**—transferring the data recorded in the journal to the ledger. The data are thereby classified by accounts in the ledger (i.e., separate accounts for each asset, liability, and element of owners' equity).

5. **Prepare a trial balance** from the ledger.

6. **Prepare financial statements.**

7-11. The other phases of the accounting cycle are discussed in Chapter 5.

B. Explanation of each phase.

1. Raw data collection is the initial step in the accounting information processing cycle. The raw data (and the supporting or source documents) that enter the accounting system are not generated by the accounting function but by various operating functions of the business.

   Jan. 2—Sale of merchandise to a customer on account, $3,000; the source document is the charge bill.

   Jan. 3—Investment of $10,000 cash in the business by the owners; source document is the cash receipt and stock (nopar) issuance records.

2. Transaction analysis is a mental process whereby the economic effects on the entity of each transaction are determined in terms of the basic accounting model: Assets = Liabilities + Owners' Equity.

To illustrate, transaction analysis of the two transactions in B above would be:

Jan. 2—Sale of merchandise on credit: Accounts receivable increase (debit), $3,000, and Sales revenue recognized (credit), $3,000.

Jan. 3—Investment by owners; Cash increase (debit), $10,000, and owners' equity, Capital stock, increase (debit), $10,000.

3. The **journal** is an accounting record designed for recording the dual effect of each business transaction in order of date; that is, in the *chronological order* in which they occur. Therefore, the two transactions analyzed on the previous page would be recorded in the journal (i.e., journalized) as follows:

JOURNAL Page 13

DATE		ACCOUNT TITLES AND EXPLANATION	FO-LIO	DEBIT	CREDIT
Jan.	2	Accounts receivable	110	3 0 0 0	
		Sales revenue	700		3 0 0 0
		To record a sale on credit.			
Jan.	3	Cash	101	1 0 0 0 0	
		Capital stock, no par	600		1 0 0 0 0
		To record investment by owners.			

Observe that the account credited and the amount credited both are "indented" from the debits. This arrangement is for convenience and to help prevent errors in recording. The process of entering a transaction in the journal is called **journalizing**.

4. The **ledger** is the name given to the accounting record that contains all of the accounts for the assets, liabilities, and owners' equity (see above).

Each transaction is transferred from the journal to the ledger (the accounts). This procedure is called **posting**. Posting of the above two transactions would be accomplished as follows:

Cash			#101
Jan. 3	13	10,000	

Capital Stock			#600
	Jan. 3	13	10,000

Accounts Receivable			#110
Jan. 2	13	3,000	

Sales Revenue			#700
	Jan. 2	13	3,000

You should observe that the page number of the journal (13) is also posted to the ledger accounts and that the ledger account numbers (101, 110, 600, and 700) are entered in the journal (folio columns). These are called "folio numbers" and are used (a) to indicate that the posting was completed and (b) as a reference for future tracing should there be errors or for other reasons. This procedure often is called "providing an audit trail."

5. A **trial balance** is prepared at the end of each accounting period; it is a list of all of the accounts shown in the ledger along with the balance (dollar amount) in each account. In a trial balance the total debits will always equal the total credits in the absence of errors. It is not a financial statement; rather, it is an information processing step that leads to the financial statements.

To illustrate, a trial balance of the above ledger (assuming only the two above transactions) would appear as follows:

HYPOTHETICAL COMPANY
Trial balance
December 31, 19XX

Acct. No.	Account Title	Balance	
		Debit	Credit
101	Cash	10,000	
110	Accounts receivable	3,000	
600	Capital stock, no par		10,000
700	Sales revenue		3,000
-	Total	13,000	13,000

6. Financial statements—At the end of the accounting period when all transactions have been recorded (Phases 1 – 4) and the trial balance completed (Phase 5), the financial-statement phase can be completed. This phase involves preparation of the three required statements (income statement, balance sheet, and statement of cash flows) and the supporting notes. This phase is discussed later.

C. The income statement reports the different classifications of revenue and expense.

1. The revenues may be classified as sales revenue and service revenue.

2. Expenses are classified by type depending upon the nature of the business. Cost of goods sold is the amount that was incurred to purchase the merchandise that was sold during the period.

3. The principal captions on the income statement are:

Revenues:
    Sales revenue
    Service revenue
Expenses:
    Cost of goods
    Operating expenses
        Selling expenses
        General and Administrative expenses
        Interest expense
Income before extraordinary items
Extraordinary items
Net income
Earnings per share

(a) Extraordinary items are the nonoperating gains and losses of the business. They have two characteristics: (1) they are **unusual in nature** and (2) they **occur infrequently**. They are set out separately on the income statement for the benefit of the user because of their special nonoperating characteristics.

(b) A corporation is required to pay income taxes. In contrast, a sole proprietorship and partnership are not required to pay income taxes as entities separate from their owners. Income taxes are reported as an expense on the income statement of a corporation.

4. Earnings per share must be reported on the income statement of the corporation. Earnings per share is computed by dividing net income by the average number of common stock shares outstanding. For example, the computation would be:

$$\frac{\text{Net income}}{\text{Average common shares outstanding}} = \frac{\$15,000}{10,000} = \$1.50 \text{ EPS}$$

D. Assets are grouped into six different categories on the balance sheet:

1. Current assets—cash and other resources expected to be converted to cash during the coming year, or the operating cycle of the business, whichever is the longer.
2. Long-term investments and funds—investments that the company intends to hold for the long run (more than one year or the operating cycle, whichever is the longer).
3. Tangible operational or fixed assets (often called "property, plant, and equipment")—includes those assets having physical substance that are held for use in operating the business, rather than for sale.
4. Intangible operational assets—those assets having no physical substance. Their value is derived from certain rights and privileges (example, patents).
5. Deferred charges—long-term prepayments for goods and services which will be used later in operating the business.
6. Other assets—a miscellaneous asset category.

E. Liabilities are classified on the balance sheet as:

1. Current liabilities—short-term debts that will be paid out of the current assets (listed on the balance sheet) within the coming year, or the operating cycle of the business, whichever is the longer.
2. Long-term liabilities—all of the debts and obligations not classified as current liabilities.

F. For a corporation, stockholders' equity is classified on the balance sheet as:

1. Contributed capital—the sum of cash and other resources invested in the business by the owners.
2. Retained earnings—cumulative earnings less cumulative losses and less all dividends paid to stockholders.

G. Working capital is not a separate classification on the balance sheet but is an important concept. The computation is: Working capital = Current assets − Current liabilities.

H. Subclassifications on the Statement of Cash flows (SCF):

   1. Cash flows from operating activities
   2. Cash flows from investing activities
   3. Cash flows from financing activities

3—Questions for Self Evaluation

These questions follow the sequence of the discussions in the chapter. However, they do not cover all of the points discussed in the chapter. After studying the chapter, try to answer each question to the best of your ability without referring again to the chapter. After answering all of them, turn to the solutions in the back and evaluate yourself. This should provide a valuable guide for deciding how much additional study you should commit to the chapter.

1. Match the records listed to the right with the definitions given to the left by entering the appropriate letter to the left:

   (a) _____ The record that has a different account for each asset, liability, and element of owners' equity.

         A. Journal
         B. Trial balance
         C. Ledger

   (b) _____ A listing of the accounts (by title) and the respective debit or credit balances.

   (c) _____ The record of all transactions, as analyzed, in chronological order.

2. Recording transactions in the journal is usually called _____ , whereas transferring data from the journal to the ledger is known as _____ .

3. The journal is sometimes called the book of _____ , whereas the ledger is sometimes called the book of _____ .

4. Transaction analysis (of an exchange transaction) usually follows the journalizing and posting phases of the accounting processing cycle. _____ T; _____ F

5. The steps in the information processing cycle discussed in the chapter are listed below in random order. You are to indicate their sequential order of completion by numbering them in the consecutive order listed in the chapter.

   (a) _____ Journalizing   (d) _____ Posting

   (b) _____ Financial statements   (e) _____ Trial balance

   (c) _____ Transaction analysis   (f) _____ Raw data collection (source documents)

6. The folio column is included primarily to provide a cross reference (i.e., audit trail) between the

   (a) _____ and the (b) _____ .

7. The two primary purposes of a trial balance are to:

   (a) _____

   (b) _____

8. If a trial balance does not balance (i.e., debits do not equal credits) it indicates that the business suffered a net loss. _____ T; _____ F.

9. Financial statements prepared for investors, creditors, and other statement users include subclassifications of the information presented in order to assist the decision makers in _____ _____ .

10. Following is a scrambled list of the usual subclassifications on an income statement. Number them in the customary order.

_____ EPS   _____ Income before extraordinary items

_____ Cost of goods sold   _____ Net income

_____ Revenues   _____ Extraordinary items

_____ Expenses other than
        cost of goods sold

11. Cost of goods sold is _____ .

12. Extraordinary gains and losses are defined in accounting as items that are both (a) _____ _____ and (b) _____ .

13. On the income statement of a corporation, income tax expense must be reported in two parts when there are extraordinary items; the two parts are:

(a) _____

(b) _____

14. Complete the following partial income statement amounts for a retail business.

Sales revenue.. $100,000

(a) _____ 60,000

Operating expenses ....(b) _____
Net income .... $ 15,000

15. The income statement for Bryce Corporation at December 31, 19B, reported the following:

Income before extraordinary items $27,000
Extraordinary loss $10,000
    Less income tax saving.................   4,000
Net income $21,000

Assuming 30,000 shares of common stock were outstanding on December 31, 19B, compute the earnings per share: _____

16. X Corporation reported pretax income of $50,000 and an extraordinary item of $10,000. Assuming a 30 percent income tax rate which applied to all items, total income tax expenses would be:

(a) Assuming an extraordinary gain $ _____ .

(b) Assuming an extraordinary loss $ _____ .

17. A calendar year income statement should be dated "At December 31, 19A". _____ T; _____ F

18. The annual accounting year for businesses always ends on December 31. _____ T; _____ F

19. Liquidity means nearness to cash; that is, the average time required to convert a noncash item to cash. _____ T; _____ F

20. A calendar year balance sheet should be dated "For the year ended December 31, 19XX." _____ T; _____ F

21. Extraordinary items are not reported as such on the balance sheet. _____ T; _____ F

22. The classification on the income statement for nonoperating gains and losses, that is, those that are unusual in nature and infrequent in occurrence, is called _____ .

23. Complete the following skeleton balance sheet so that it reflects the classifications in the order that they are usually used.

Balance Sheet

Assets

Current assets

(a) _____

(b) _____

(c) _____

(d) _____

(e) _____

Liabilities

(f) _____

(g) _____

Stockholders' Equity

(h) _____

(i) _____

(j) _____

24. Current assets are listed on the balance sheet in order of their _____ , which is the average time required to convert a noncash resource to cash.

25. The connecting link between the income statement and owners' equity on the balance sheet is the

_____ .

26. Match each of the following accounting terms with its proper definition by inserting the letter which identifies the definition in the space next to the term.

Accounting Terms

_____ (1) Accounting information processing cycle

_____ (2) Accounting period

_____ (3) Cost of goods sold

_____ (4) Current assets

_____ (5) Current liabilities

_____ (6) Extraordinary items

_____ (7) Journal entry

_____ (8) Ledger

_____ (9) Operating cycle

_____ (10) Operational assets

_____ (11) Posting

_____ (12) Trial balance

_____ (13) Working capital

Definitions

A. A gain or loss that is unusual and infrequent; separately reported on the income statement

B. An expense that represents the cost of purchasing merchandise that was sold during the accounting period

C. Time-period; usually one year; the period covered by the financial statements

D. Assets used to operate a business; not for resale; often called "property, plant and equipment"

E. Sequential accounting phases used to process data from initial transaction to financial statements

F. A list of all of the accounts in the ledger and their balances

G. Used to define current assets and current liabilities; the time from cash to purchase of inventory; to sale on credit, and back to cash

H. An original entry made in the journal in terms of: A = L + OE and Debits = Credits

I. Contains all of the individual accounts for assets, liabilities, and owners' equity

J. Assets that are expected to be converted to cash within one year or the operating cycle if longer

K. Liabilities that will be paid by using current assets within one year or the operating cycle if longer

L. Difference between total current assets and total current liabilities

M. Transferring data from the journal to the ledger

4

Adjusting Entries and the Conceptual Framework of Accounting

PURPOSE OF THIS CHAPTER

Chapter 3 discussed the accounting information processing cycle. A primary purpose of Chapter 4 is to continue the development of the accounting cycle by introducing a group of entries called *adjusting* entries. These entries are made at the end of each reporting period so that the revenue and expenses can be properly measured for the period.

This chapter also introduces the conceptual framework of accounting which will help you understand *why* certain accounting procedures are used.

HOW TO STUDY THIS CHAPTER

This chapter considers the matching of expenses with revenues which is necessary to measure periodic net income. It will require more study than the average chapter. You should focus on the measurement approaches used in deriving net income: that is, (1) when revenues are recognized as earned (i.e., identified with a particular accounting period) and (2) how the expenses are matched with the revenues of the period. A clear understanding of the revenue and matching principles is essential. In this respect you should devote special study to the adjusting entries because they implement these two principles. A good understanding of the conceptual framework will help you answer questions that arise in subsequent chapters.

STUDY OUTLINE OF THIS CHAPTER

Part A—Adjusting Entries

A. Accrual accounting—completed transactions are recorded when they occur, regardless of when any related cash receipts or payments occur. Accrual accounting is required by GAAP.

   1. Revenue principle—revenue is recorded when it is earned, not necessarily when it is collected in cash.

2. Matching principle—expenses are recorded in the same accounting period as the revenue they helped generate.

B. Adjusting Entries—some transactions overlap two or more accounting periods. In these cases, journal entries must be made at the end of each accounting period to reflect the effects of the transactions.

1. There are four types of transactions that result in adjusting entries:

   (a) Revenue collected in advance but not yet earned (called deferred revenue).
   (b) Revenue earned but not yet collected (called accrued revenue).
   (c) Expenses paid in advance (called deferred expense).
   (d) Expenses incurred but not paid (called accrued expense).

C. Four different situations in which adjusting entries are made are illustrated below assuming the accounting year ends December 31:

1. Expenses incurred prior to payment (accrued expense)—items for which the enterprise recognizes an expense before the related cash is paid (i.e., payment is in a subsequent accounting period).

   Example: At the end of 19B it is determined that wages to employees of $1,000 have been earned but neither recorded nor paid. At December 31, 19B, the following adjusting entry must be made to record the expense and the liability:

Wage expense	1,000	
Wages payable (a liability)		1,000

2. Revenues earned prior to collection (accrued revenue)—items for which the enterprise recognizes a revenue before the related cash is collected (i.e., collection is in a subsequent accounting period).

   Example: At the end of 19B it is determined that commissions earned amounting to $500 have not been recorded nor collected. At December 31, 19B, the following adjusting entry must be made to record the revenue earned and to record the asset:

Commissions receivable (an asset)	500	
Commission revenue		500

3. Expenses paid in advance (deferred or prepaid expense)—items for which the company recognizes expense after the related cash is paid (i.e., payment was made in a prior accounting period).

Example: A two-year insurance premium of $200 was paid on January 1, 19B. This was recorded at that date as a debit to prepaid insurance (an asset account) and as a credit to cash. At December 31, 19B, the following adjusting entry is required to apportion the cost and to reduce the asset account:

Insurance expense..................................	100	
Prepaid insurance		100

4. Revenue collected in advance (deferred revenue)—items for which the enterprise recognizes revenue after the related cash is collected (i.e., collection was made in a prior accounting period).

Example: At the end of 19B it was determined that on December 1, 19B, rent had been collected from a customer amounting to $800 which was for December 19B and January 19C. The entry made on that date debited cash for $800 and credited rent revenue for $800. At December 31, 19B, the following adjusting entry would have to be made to reduce the 19B rent revenue and to record the liability for the one month's rent collected in advance:

Rent revenue	400	
Rent revenue collected in advance or unearned rent revenue (a liability)		400

5. Some adjusting entries must be based on estimates. Examples are (a) the adjusting entry for depreciation expense (resulting from an expense prepayment or deferral when the related asset was purchased, see E, 3, (b) above); and (b) the adjusting entry for bad debt expense (an expense accrual) which is illustrated later.

D. Adjusting entries are recorded in the journal and dated the last day of the period (e.g., in the above illustrations, December 31, 19B) and are posted immediately to the ledger accounts.

Part B—Conceptual Framework of Accounting

E. The Financial Accounting Standards Board has published a series of statements of accounting concepts which set forth its view of the conceptual framework.

F. Essential Characteristics of Accounting Information:

    2. Accounting information should help decision makers make better decisions. Useful information must be:

      (a) Relevant—capable of influencing decisions.

      (b) Reliable—current and verifiable

    3. A secondary characteristic of accounting information is comparability which means that information concerning one company should be comparable with other companies.

    4. The cost-benefit constraint states that the cost of preparing information should not exceed its value to decision makers.

G. Fundamental Concepts of Accounting

Assumptions of Accounting:

    1. Separate entity assumption—each business must be accounted for separate and apart from its owners and other entities.

    2. Continuity assumption—a business is assumed to have an indefinite life.

    3. Unit-of-measure assumption—each entity will account for its financial results in terms of the national monetary unit.

4. Time period assumption—decision makers require timely information which means that business entities should prepare financial reports at least once a year.

H. Principles of Accounting

1. Cost principle—all financial statement elements should be recorded at their cash-equivalent cost.

2. Revenue principle—revenue should be recorded when there is an inflow of assets from the sale of goods or services.

3. Matching principle—all of the expenses incurred in earning revenue should be reported in the same period that the related revenue is reported.

4. Full-disclosure principle—a business must report all of the relevant information about the economic affairs of a business.

I. Constraints of Accounting

1. Materiality threshold—immaterial items do not have to be separately reported.

2. Cost-benefit constraint—the cost of preparing information should not exceed its value to decision makers.

3. Conservatism constraint—businesses should avoid overstating assets and revenues, and understating liabilities and expenses.

J. Elements of Financial Statements—broad classifications of information that should be reported.

    1. Income Statement

        (a) Revenues
        (b) Expenses
        (c) Gains
        (d) Losses

    2. Balance Sheet

        (a) Assets
        (b) Liabilities
        (c) Owners' equity

K. Practices and Procedures of Accounting—the practical guidelines used to implement accounting concepts.

4—Questions for Self Evaluation

These questions follow the sequence of the discussions in the chapter. However, they do not cover all of the points discussed in the chapter. After studying the chapter, try to answer each question to the best of your ability without referring again to the chapter. After answering all of them, turn to the solutions in the back and evaluate yourself. This should provide a valuable guide for deciding how much additional study you should commit to the chapter.

1. After the adjusting entry for year 2, for depreciation on a truck (used in the business and a 5 year estimated life) the depreciation expense and accumulated depreciation accounts will reflect identical balances. _____ T; _____ F

2. The _____ principle holds that all of the expenses incurred in generating revenue should be identified with the revenue generated, period by period.

3. Company B paid $3,600 cash for a three-year insurance premium on July 1, 19B; the policy expires on June 30, 19E. The accounting year ends on December 31. How much insurance expense should be reported in 19B? $ _____ ; in 19C? $ _____ .

4. For each independent situation provide the dollar amounts by year (accounting period ends December 31):

Situation	19A	19B	19C
(a) Depreciation each full year on a machine is $6,000; the machine was acquired on July 1, 19A. Depreciation expense would be:	$	$	$
(b) For item (a), the balance in the Accumulated depreciation account at the end of each year would be:			
(c) On July 1, 19A, paid a two-year insurance premium (insurance on company assets), $4,800 (debit to Prepaid insurance). Insurance expense for this policy would be:			
(d) For item (c), the balance in the prepaid insurance account at the end of each year would be:			
(e) On September 1, 19B, collected rent revenue for six months in advance, $2,400 (credit to Rent revenue). Rent revenue would be:			
(f) For item (e), the balance in the account, Rent revenue collected in advance, at the end of each year, would be:			
(g) On July 1, 19A, a two-year interest-bearing (12%) note payable of $10,000 was signed; therefore, interest expense for a full year would be $1,200. Interest expense would be:			
(h) For item (g), the balance in the account, Interest payable at the end of each year, assuming interest is paid each June 30, would be:			

5. At the end of 19X it was determined property taxes for the period July 1, 19X, to June 30, 19Y, of $4,800 have not been recorded or paid (due date is July 1, 19Y). Give the required adjusting entry at December 31, 19X, and indicate in the entry the types of accounts debited and credited.

_____ _____ _____
_____ _____ _____
_____ _____ _____

6. On July 1, 19A, Company X paid a $1,200 insurance premium on its equipment. The premium was for two years in advance. The entry was recorded as follows:

    July 1, 19A:
        Prepaid insurance   1,200
        Cash   1,200

Required:

(a) Give the adjusting entry that would be required on December 31, 19A (end of the annual accounting period).

_____ _____ _____
_____ _____ _____
_____ _____ _____

(b) Explain briefly the two purposes that the adjusting entry served.

(1) _____
_____
_____

(2) _____
_____
_____

7. On October 1, 19A, Company T borrowed $10,000 on a one-year, 12 percent interest-bearing note. At maturity date, September 30, 19B, the company will pay the note principal, $10,000 plus interest for one year ($10,000 × 12% = $1,200); a total of $11,200. The note was recorded as follows:

    October 1, 19A:
        Cash   10,000
        Note payable, 12%   10,000

Required:

(a) Give the required adjusting entry for interest on December 31, 19A (end of the annual accounting period).

_____ _____ _____
_____ _____ _____
_____ _____ _____

8. Immediately below is a list of account titles. Each account has been given a code letter in parentheses to the left.

(a) Prepaid insurance
(b) Depreciation expense
(c) Maintenance expense
(d) Accumulated depreciation
(e) Accrued wages payable
(f) Interest payable
(g) Rent revenue

(h) Inventory of maintenance supplies
(i) Insurance expense
(j) Wage expense
(k) Cash
(l) Interest expense
(m) Rent collected in advance
(n) Rent revenue receivable

On the following page is a list of transactions; each one requires an adjusting entry at the end of the period, December 31, 19A. All amounts needed are given; however, you are to verify each. Also, to the right you are to indicate by code letters the accounts that should be debited and credited in each adjusting entry at December 31, 19A. The first transaction is given as an example.

Transactions	December 31, 19A Adjusting Entry Debit	Credit
(1) On January 1, 19A, the company paid a two-year insurance premium. The entry was debit Prepaid insurance, $400; credit Cash, $400. Therefore, the adjusting entry at December 31, 19A, will be for the $200. Example.	Verification: $400 × 12/24 = $200.	
	i	a
(2) The company owned a truck that cost $4,000. It has an estimated useful life of five years. Therefore, the adjusting entry at December 31, 19A, will be for $800.		
(3) During the year maintenance supplies that cost $400 were purchased and placed in the supply room to be used as needed. The $400 was debited to Inventory of maintenance supplies when purchased. The beginning inventory of supplies was $20. At the end of the year, December 31, there were unused supplies amounting to $100; therefore, the adjusting entry will be for $320.		
(4) At December 31, 19A, wages of $700, althrough earned by the employees, were unrecorded and unpaid. Therefore, an adjusting entry must be made for this amount.		
(5) The company owed a $2,000, 12 percent one-year note payable dated July 1, 19A. The $240 interest is payable on due date, June 30, 19B. Therefore, an adjusting entry for six months interest of $120 must be made on December 31, 19A.		
(6) On December 1, 19A, the company collected $2,400 rent revenue for three months (through February 28, 19B). The collection of cash was debited to Cash and credited to Rent collected in advance. Therefore, an adjusting entry must be made for $800.		
(7) On December 31, 19A, one tenant had failed to pay the rent for November and December amounting to $400 per month. Therefore, an adjusting entry must be made for this amount.		

9. On January 1, 19A, Blue Company purchased equipment for use in the business which cost $10,000. The equipment has an estimated useful life of eight years and an estimated residual value of $400 (assume straight-line depreciation).

(a) Give the required adjusting entry at December 31, 19B (end of the annual accounting period).

_____ _____ _____

_____ _____ _____

_____ _____ _____

(b) What two purposes does the above adjusting entry serve?

(1) _____

_____

(2) _____

_____

_____

(c) After the above adjusting entry, what would be the balance of the accumulated depreciation account? Why is it called a contra account?

_____

_____

_____

(d) What is the *book value* of the asset at the end of 19A? $ _____ ;
19B? $ _____ .

10. On September 1, 19A, Bock Company loaned $1,000 cash on a one-year, 15 percent interest-bearing note receivable. The interest is payable on the due date of the note, August 31, 19B. The note was recorded as follows:

September 1, 19A:
  Note receivable 1,000
    Cash 1,000

Give the adjusting entry for interest required on December 31, 19A (end of the annual accounting period).

_____ _____ _____

_____ _____ _____

_____ _____ _____

11. At the end of 19A, there were unpaid wages of $850 that had been earned during December 19A and had not been recorded.

   (a) Give the adjusting entry required at December 31, 19A (end of the annual accounting period):

   _____ _____ _____

   _____ _____ _____

   _____ _____ _____

   (b) What two purposes are served by the above adjusting entry?

      (1) _____

          _____

      (2) _____

          _____

          _____

12. The two required financial statements that report the "changes" between the beginning and ending balance sheets are the:

   (a) _____

   (b) _____

13. Dividing of the life span of a business into relatively short time periods for accounting measuring and reporting purposes is based upon what usually is called the _____ assumption.

14. Financial statements prepared for time periods of less than one year (such as quarterly statements) usually are referred to as _____ statements.

15. Entries made at the end of the period, to implement the matching principle, which serve to better measure net income by changing certain account balances usually are called _____ .

16. The matching principle takes precedence over the revenue principle. _____ T; _____ F

17. XT Service Company started a service job for a customer on December 19, 19W and completed the job on January 3, 19X. XT Company billed the customer for $600 (total price) on January 4, 19X; therefore, the entire amount should be recognized as 19X revenue. _____ T; _____ F

18. Under the accrual basis, recognition of revenue and the related cash collection always coincide.

   _____ T; _____ F

19. Accumulated depreciation is a *contra* asset account. _____ T; _____ F

20. Rent revenue collected in advance is reported on the balance sheet as a liability. _____ T; _____ F

21. Four underlying assumptions of accounting are: (a) _____ ,

   (b) _____ , (c) _____ ,

   and (d) _____ .

(b) _____ , (c) _____ ,

and (d) _____ .

23. The _____ constraint states that the cost of preparing information should not exceed its value to decision makers.

24. _____ means that information is capable of influencing decisions.

25. _____ means that information is correct and verifiable.

26. Match each of the following accounting terms with its proper definition by inserting the letter which identifies the definition in the space next to the term.

Accounting Terms

_____ (1) Accrue (accrued)

_____ (2) Adjusting entries

_____ (3) Conservatism constraint

_____ (4) Contra account

_____ (5) Cost benefit constraint

_____ (6) Defer (deferred)

_____ (7) Depreciation

_____ (8) Elements of financial statements

_____ (9) Expenses paid in advance

_____ (10) Expenses unpaid (accrued expenses)

_____ (11) Fiscal year

_____ (12) Interest expense

_____ (13) Interim reports

_____ (14) Matching principle

_____ (15) Reliability principle

_____ (16) Residual value

_____ (17) Revenue collected in advance

_____ (18) Revenue earned but not yet collected or recorded

_____ (19) Revenue principle

_____ (20) Supplies inventory

_____ (21) Time-period assumption

Definitions

A. An expense paid in advance of use; a revenue collected in advance of earning.

B. End-of-period entries required by the revenue and matching principles to attain a cutoff between periods.

C. Time value of money; the cost of borrowing money (or other assets acquired)

D. All costs incurred to earn the revenues of the period must be identified then matched with the revenue by recording as expense

E. Revenue not yet collected, or recorded, but already earned. Accrued revenue.

F. An account, related to a primary account, that is an offset (or reduction) to the primary account

G. Value (estimated) of an operational asset at the end of its useful life to the business (scrap or salvage value)

H. Supplies purchased and still on hand; unused supplies at the end of the period.

I. Financial reports for periods of less than one year; quarterly or monthly reports.

J. An expense incurred but not yet paid; a revenue earned but not yet collected

K. An accounting period of twelve months that does not end on December 31.

L. Division of the operating activities of a business into a series of equal time periods (usually one year) for accounting purposes.

M. Expense of using (wearing out) a building, machinery, fixtures, etc., each period of useful life

N. Recognize revenue in the period earned rather than when the cash is received; earnings process completed.

O. Expenses actually incurred but not yet paid or recorded.

P. Cash paid for goods, or services, before those goods or services are used; prepaid expenses.

Q. Revenue collected in cash before that revenue is earned. Precollected revenue.

R. Financial statements must be unbiased, accurate, and verifiable.

S. Do not overstate assets and revenues or understate liabilities and expenses.

T. All assets, liabilities, and owners' equity items are recorded initially at cost.

U. Major classifications on financial statements.

Information Processing in an Accounting System

PURPOSE OF THIS CHAPTER

Chapter 3 introduced the accounting information processing cycle and Chapter 4 discussed an important phase of the cycle—adjusting entries. The purpose of Chapter 5 is to expand and complete the cycle. The expansion in this chapter involves additional phases that are performed at the end of the accounting (i.e., reporting) year. Accounting worksheets, adjusting entries, closing entries, and financial statements are emphasized. A clear understanding of this chapter will help you learn more applications of the: (a) conceptual framework of accounting, and (b) accounting information processing cycle.

HOW TO STUDY THIS CHAPTER

This chapter focuses on the flow of information through an accounting system. It expands on the information processing system introduced in Chapter 3 and incorporates the issues discussed in Chapter 4. In studying this chapter, you should focus on the sequential steps comprising the information processing cycle that is repeated each accounting period. It is essential that you carefully study the continuing illustrations given in the chapter.

STUDY OUTLINE OF THIS CHAPTER

A.   Information processing of accounting data usually involves a combination of three different approaches:

1.   Manual data processing—The work is done by hand.
2.   Mechanical data processing—The work is done by using specially designed machines.
3.   Computerized data processing—The work is done by means of computers.

B.   Accounting information processing cycle—This cycle was introduced in Chapter 3, Part A. In that discussion six phases were introduced. In this chapter four more phases are presented which complete the entire processing cycle. They are: Preparation of an accounting worksheet, recording the adjusting entries, recording the closing entries, and preparation of a post-closing trial balance.

C. The complete accounting information processing cycle includes the following ten sequential phases (those added in this chapter are indicated with an asterisk).

Phases completed throughout each annual accounting period:

1. **Collection of raw economic data**—as each transaction is completed, the source documents are collected and transmitted to the accounting function.

2. **Transaction analysis**—a mental activity that identifies and measures the economic impact of the transaction in terms of the fundamental accounting model (Assets = Liabilities + Owners' Equity).

3. **Journalizing**—the process of recording in the journal, in chronological order, the results of Phase 2 (for each transaction).

4. **Posting**—transferring the data recorded in the journal to the ledger. The data are thereby classified by accounts in the ledger (i.e., separate accounts for each asset, liability, and element of owners' equity).

Phases completed at the end of each annual accounting period:

5. **Prepare an unadjusted trial balance**—at the end of the period, the balance of each account in the ledger is listed on the trial balance. It is called **unadjusted** because the adjusting entries have not yet been recorded.

*6. **Prepare a worksheet** (to develop the income statement, statement of retained earnings, and balance sheet)—this is an optional phase which facilitates completion of all of the subsequent phases.

   This worksheet is prepared by (a) entering thereon the unadjusted trial balance (Phase 5); next, (b) the adjusting entries are entered thereon; and finally (c) each amount (as adjusted) is extended horizontally on the worksheet to the income statement, statement of retained earnings, or balance sheet columns (i.e., revenues and expenses to the income statement columns, net income and dividends paid to the statement of retained earnings columns, and assets, liabilities, and owners' equity to the balance sheet columns).

Important—study Exhibits 5-2 and 5-3 in the textbook.

7. **Prepare financial statements**—the income statement, statement of retained earnings, and balance sheet are prepared from the data shown on the completed worksheet (Phase 6). Note—financial statements usually are prepared at this point because businesses want to issue the statements as quickly as possible. This phase can be completed after any of the later phases.

*8. **Adjusting entries**—the adjusting entries reflected in the worksheet (Phase 6) are recorded in the journal and then posted to the ledger. This phase brings the account balances into agreement with those reported on the financial statements (Phase 7). Study Exhibit 5-4 in the textbook.

*9. **Closing entries**—all of the revenue and expense accounts are closed which means that their balances are transferred to the Income summary account; this account is then closed to Retained earnings. The closing entries are recorded in the journal and immediately posted to the ledger. After posting, only the asset, liability, and owners' equity accounts (but not the revenue and expense accounts) will reflect balances. Also Dividends paid is closed to Retained earnings. This process prepares the accounts for the start of the next accounting period. That is, the income statement accounts (revenues and expenses) start the next period with zero balances and the balance sheet accounts (assets, liabilities, and owners' equity) start the next period with the same amounts that are reported on the current balance sheet. Study Exhibit 5-5 in the text.

*10. **Preparation of a post-closing trial balance**—this trial balance is prepared to check the equality of the debit and credit balances in the ledger after the adjusting and closing entries have been posted. Note that only the balance sheet accounts will have amounts in this trial balance because all of the income statement accounts will have been closed.

11. **Optional reversing entries**. The purpose of reversing entries is to facilitate recording subsequent related entries. Study Exhibit 5-7 in the text.

D. Interim financial statements. These are statements for a reporting period of less than one year (e.g., quarterly statements).

5—Questions for Self Evaluation

These questions follow the sequence of the discussions in the chapter. However, they do not cover all of the points discussed in the chapter. After studying the chapter, try to answer each question to the best of your ability without referring again to the chapter. After answering all of them, turn to the solutions in the back and evaluate yourself. This should provide a valuable guide for deciding how much additional study you should commit to the chapter.

1. In computerized data processing, the computer and the other machines related to it usually are referred to as the _____; the computer programs and instructions are called the _____ .

2. Indicate the sequential order of the ten phases of the information processing cycle by numbering in the spaces to the left.

   _____ (a) Closing entries

   _____ (b) Financial statements

   _____ (c) Journalizing

   _____ (d) Worksheet

   _____ (e) Posting

   _____ (f) Post-closing trial balance

   _____ (g) Collection of raw economic data

   _____ (h) Adjusting entries

   _____ (i) Unadjusted trial balance

   _____ (j) Transaction analysis

3. A worksheet is considered to be one phase of the accounting information processing cycle because it is required. _____ T; _____ F

4. Adjusting entries are: (a) entered on the worksheet, (b) recorded in the journal, and (c) posted to the ledger. _____ T; _____ F

5. The amounts entered in the first pair of debit/credit columns of the worksheet are obtained from the _____.

6. The worksheet can be completed at any time during the current accounting period. _____ T; _____ F

7. The completed worksheet provides the essential data for preparation of the following financial statements:

   (a) _____

   (b) _____

   (c) _____

8. The closing entries are recorded in the (a) _____ and posted to the

   (b) _____ .

9. At the end of the annual accounting period, December 31, 19A, the following accounting data were available for Nest Corporation: retained earnings, January 1, 19A, $20,000; dividends declared and paid during 19A, $12,000; net income for 19A, $15,000.

   (a) Prepare a statement of retained earnings for 19A.
   (b) What amount(s) from the statement will be shown on the 19A balance sheet?
   (c) Give two closing entries indicated by the above amounts.

10. The balance sheet accounts often are called the _____ accounts, and the income statement accounts are called the _____ accounts.

11. The _____ accounts are closed at the end of each accounting period; whereas the _____ accounts are not closed at the end of each accounting period.

12. Each amount (shown on the worksheet) in the first pair of debit/credit columns (as adjusted) is extended to both the income statement and balance sheet columns (assume no columns for retained earnings). _____ T; _____ F

13. The real and nominal accounts are closed at the end of each annual accounting period. _____ T; _____ F

14. All revenue accounts are closed by recording a closing entry which debits (a) _____ , and credits (b) _____ .

15. Thomas Corporation is completing the annual information processing cycle at December 31, 19B, end of the annual accounting period. The accounts reflect the following balances:

	Debits			Credits
(a) Cash	$ 5,000	(h)	Allowance for doubtful accounts	$ 1,000
(b) Accounts receivable	8,000	(i)	Accumulated depreciation	2,000
(c) Equipment	15,000	(j)	Accounts payable	7,000
(d) Inventory (perpetual)	4,000	(k)	Bonds payable	10,000
(e) Other assets	21,000	(l)	Capital stock	20,000
(f) Expenses (including		(m)	Retained earnings	8,000
income taxes)	20,000	(n)	Revenues	30,000
(g) Dividends declared and paid	5,000	(o)	Income summary	
	$78,000			$78,000

Use the journal below to record all of the closing entries required at December 31, 19B, end of the annual accounting period.

JOURNAL

DATE	ACCOUNT TITLES AND EXPLANATION	FO-LIO	DEBIT	CREDIT

16. Match each of the following accounting terms with its proper definition by inserting the letter which identifies the definition in the space next to the term.

Accounting Terms

_____ (1) Accounting information processing cycle

_____ (2) Closing entries

_____ (3) Computer hardware

_____ (4) Computer software

_____ (5) Computerized data processing

_____ (6) Manual data processing

_____ (7) Mechanical data processing

_____ (8) Permanent (real) accounts

_____ (9) Post-closing trial balance

_____ (10) Reversing entries

_____ (11) Temporary (nominal) accounts

_____ (12) Worksheet

Definitions

A. Computer and other equipment used with it

B. Income statement accounts; closed at the end of the accounting period

C. Accounting process performed (in whole or in part) in handwriting; manually

D. Accounting phases (steps) from the time a transaction is completed to the financial statements

E. Trial balance prepared after all of the closing entries have been posted

F. Accounting process performed (in whole or in part) using electronic computers

G. A "spread sheet" designed to minimize errors and to provide data for the financial statements

H. Computer programs and instructions for using an electronic computer

I. Permanent (or real) accounts are the balance sheet accounts; no closing entries

J. End-of-period entries to close all revenue and expense accounts to retained earnings (through income summary)

K. Recorded at beginning of next accounting period; backs out certain reversing entries; facilitates subsequent entries

L. Accounting process performed (in whole or in part) using machines

Accounting for Sales Revenue and Cost of Goods Sold

PURPOSE OF THIS CHAPTER

The previous five chapters discussed the various phases of the information processing cycle and the conceptual framework of accounting. In this chapter, you will apply that knowledge by examining typical business transactions that involve the purchase and sale of merchandise. Net income reported on the Income Statement is a measure of the operating success of a business. As a result, proper recording of sales revenue and the related cost of goods sold is important to both managers and users of financial statements.

HOW TO STUDY THIS CHAPTER

This chapter introduces (a) measuring, recording in the information processing system, and reporting of sales and service activities; and (b) determining of the dollar amounts of cost of goods sold (an expense) and the inventory of goods on hand at the end of the accounting period. The distinction between the **perpetual** and **periodic** inventory systems is important. You should follow the illustrations in the chapter carefully. It is particularly important to study the Demonstration Case and the recommended solution. It presents the two inventory systems in the broader context of the business. The accounting worksheet is not new to you (Chapter 5); however, you should focus on how cost of goods sold and the inventories are handled on it. A good grounding in this chapter is essential to understanding the discussions that follow in Chapter 7.

STUDY OUTLINE OF THIS CHAPTER

Part A—Accounting for Sales Revenue

A. For most businesses, selling and purchasing activities constitute a large part of their operations during each period.

1. Selling activities are reflected on the income statement as sales revenue (which requires application of the **revenue principle**) and selling expenses (which require application of the **matching principle**).

2. Purchasing activities are reflected on the income statement as cost of goods sold and on the balance sheet as inventories. These activities involve application of the **cost** and **matching principles**.

B. Accounting for sales involves sales revenue, sales returns, sales discounts, and bad debts.

1. Under the revenue principle, (a) sales revenue is reported in the period in which the sales are made; that is when ownership to the goods passes to the customer, and (b) the dollar amount recorded is the cash equivalent of the consideration received. Sales revenue, (assuming one-third on credit terms) is be recorded as follows:

Cash	20,000	
Accounts receivable	10,000	
Sales revenue		30,000

2. Sales returns and allowances occur when a customer returns goods. The journal entry to record a sales return or allowance is (assuming a periodic inventory system):

Sales returns and allowances*.....................	100	
Accounts receivable (or Cash)		100

   *On the income statement the balance of this account is subtracted from gross sales revenue.

C. Sales discounts are reductions granted to customers for early payment of amounts owed (for goods sold to the customers on credit). Goods often are sold on credit terms such as: 3/10, n/60. These terms mean that the customer will be granted a 3 percent discount if the bill is collected in 10 days; otherwise, the full amount is due within 60 days.

1. The preferred method for recording sales revenue is called the **net method**.

   (a) Assume a customer is sold goods on credit for $100 with the terms 3/10, n/60 and that the bill is collected on the ninth day. The journal entries to record the sale and subsequent collection under the **net method** are:

Accounts receivable	97	
Sales revenue ($100 × 97%)		97
To record sale on credit (at net of discount)		

Cash	97	
Accounts receivable		97
To record collection within the discount period.		

56

(b)   Assume instead that the customer does not pay the receivable within the 10-day discount period. The journal entry is:

Cash	100	
Accounts receivable		97
Interest revenue (or interest revenue earned)		3
To record collection after the discount period.		

2. An alternative method for recording sales revenue is called the gross method.

   (a) Assume a customer is sold goods on credit for $100 with terms 3/10, n/60 and that the bill is collected on the ninth day. The journal entries to record the sale and subsequent collection under the **gross method** are:

Accounts receivable	100	
Sales revenue		100
Cash ($100 × 97%)	97	
Sales discounts	3	
Accounts receivable.........................		100

   (b) Assume instead that the customer does not pay the receivable within the 10-day discount period. The journal entry is:

Cash	100	
Accounts receivable.........................		100

D. Bad debt losses are a necessary business cost associated with selling goods on credit. Occasionally a customer will not pay the bill and there is no chance of future collection. In this case there is a bad debt.

   1. Because bad debt losses usually become known (by customer name) in accounting periods after the period of the sale, such losses must be estimated in the period of the sale so that bad debt expense can be **matched** (matching principle) with the sales revenue of the period that caused the bad debt.

   2. There are two methods for measuring bad debt expense: percent of credit sales and aging of accounts receivable

   (a) *Percent of credit sales:* Assume credit sales during the period (19C) of $50,000 and an average bad debt loss rate of 1 percent of credit sales. An adjusting entry to record bad debt expense must be made at the end of the accounting period (19C) as follows:

Bad debt expense ($50,000 × 1%)	500	
Allowance for doubtful accounts.............		500

(b) *Aging of accounts receivable:* This method adjusts the balance of the allowance account based on the estimate of how many of the existing accounts receivable will be uncollectible. Assume the balance of the allowance for doubtful accounts on December 31, 19B is $500 and an analysis of accounts receivable results in an estimate that $1,200 of the accounts will be uncollectible. The journal entry to record bad debt expense is

Bad debt expense ($1,200 – $500)...............	700	
Allowance for doubtful accounts.............		700

3. The other entries used in accounting for bad debts are the same whether the percent of credit sales or aging of accounts method is used.

   (a) The Allowance for doubtful accounts is a contra or offset account to the Accounts receivable account.

   (b) A bad debt of $75 owed by J. Doe would be written off in a later accounting period, when it is determined to be uncollectible (say, in period 19D), as follows:

Allowance for doubtful accounts..........	75	
Accounts receivable (J. Doe)		75

Note that this journal entry does not affect (a) the amount of expense, or (b) the book or carrying value of net accounts receivable. To illustrate:

	Before Write-off	*After Write-off*
Accounts receivable balance*	$20,000	$19,925
Allowance for doubtful accounts balance.......	(500)	(425)
Net amount of accounts receivable	$19,500	$19,500

*($50,000 − $30,000 collected = $20,000)

E. Illustration of partial income statement (Reporting revenue, cost of goods sold, and gross margin; amounts assumed):

EXAMPLE COMPANY
INCOME STATEMENT—Partial
For the Year Ended December 31, 19E

Revenue:

Gross sales revenue	$ 94,000	
Less: Sales returns and allowances.....................	4,000	
Net sales revenue		$ 90,000
Cost of goods sold (see Part B)		32,000
Gross margin on sales		58,000

Expenses:

Etc.

Part B—Accounting for Cost of Goods Sold

F. In the illustration above, cost of goods sold, which is an expense, was subtracted from net sales in conformity with the matching principle.

1. Cost of goods sold is the amount that the company paid (i.e., cost) for all of the goods that were sold.

2. The difference between net sales revenue and cost of goods sold is called **gross margin on sales**. It can be expressed as a dollar amount (revenue – cost of goods sold) or as a percent (gross margin ÷ net sales revenue).

G. Cost of goods sold is the sum of the expenditures made to acquire the goods that were sold during the current accounting period.

1. Cost of goods sold may be computed (and reported on the income statement) as follows:

   (a) Beginning inventory (at the start of the period) ....(BI) .... $ 8,000
   (b) Add: Purchases during the period....................(P) 30,000
        Total—goods available for sale (during the period)............... 38,000
   (c) Less: Ending inventory (at the end of the period)......(EI) 6,000
        Cost of goods sold (for the period) ....(CGS) $32,000

   Cost of goods sold can be calculated as: $BI + P - EI = CGS$.

   (a) The beginning inventory (i.e., the $8,000) is known because it is carried over from the prior period; it was the ending inventory for the prior period.
   (b) The amount of purchases during the period (i.e., the $30,000) is provided by the Purchases account balance in the ledger.
   (c) Therefore, the ending inventory (i.e., $6,000) must be determined in order to compute cost of goods sold (i.e., $32,000).

H. To compute the ending inventory, a company may use either the (a) periodic inventory system, or (b) perpetual inventory system.

1. Under the **periodic inventory system** detailed inventory records are not maintained. The ending inventory is determined at the end of each period by a **physical count** of the goods remaining on hand and valued at unit cost (the $6,000 in the above example would be determined in this manner). Cost of goods sold then is computed, as above, by subtracting the ending inventory amount from the goods available for sale (i.e., $38,000 − $6,000 = $32,000).

2. Alternatively, a company may use a **perpetual inventory system**. Under this system a continuous detailed inventory record is maintained (in units and dollars) for each type of goods stocked. The record shows goods on hand at the start of the period, goods acquired during the period, and goods sold during the period. This record would show the $32,000 and $6,000 amounts given in the above example. The perpetual inventory system is excellent in most respects except that in some situations it requires a large amount of detailed, and costly, recordkeeping. However, a computer facilitates its use.

Example: A perpetual inventory record for an item stocked would look essentially like this (whether maintained by hand or by computer):

PERPETUAL INVENTORY RECORD							Item: TV Sets—Model Z1B		
	Purchased			Sold			Balance		
Date	Units	Unit Cost	Amount	Units	Unit Cost	Amount	Units	Unit Cost	Amount
Jan. 1 Inv.		$	$		$	$	2	$300	$ 600
3	10	300	3,000				12	300	3,600
7				3	300	900	9	300	2,700

End of period:
1. Cost of goods sold is the sum of this column
2. Ending inventory is the last amount in this column

I. Journal entries related to the two inventory systems. The purchases and sales entries are somewhat different when the periodic inventory system is used compared to when the perpetual inventory system is used.

1. Purchases—Assume that 10 units of a particular product are purchased at a cost of $300 per unit. The journal entry to record the purchase is:

	System		
	Periodic Inventory		Perpetual Inventory
Purchases.....................	3,000		
Merchandise inventory			3,000
Cash (or Accounts payable)......		3,000	3,000

2. Sales—Assume that three of the above units are sold for $650 each. The journal entries to record the sale under each system are:

	System		
	Periodic Inventory		Perpetual Inventory
Cash (or Accounts receivable)	1,950		1,950
Sales revenue (3 × $650)		1,950	1,950
Cost of goods sold (3 × $300)	(not determinable or		900
Merchandise inventory	recorded until the		900
	end of the period)		

3. The purchase cost recorded in journal entry (#1) is the cash equivalent amount paid less any cash discounts allowed **plus** any transportation costs paid.

   a. Cash discounts on purchases are reductions given to encourage early payment on credit purchases. Goods often are purchased on credit terms such as 2/10, n/30 (i.e., 2% discount if paid within 10 days of purchase, if not paid the toal amount is due in 30 days). The preferred method of recording purchase cash discounts is the **net method**.

   Assume goods are purchased with a cash equivalent (invoice) cost of $200 subject to the above terms. The goods are recorded as follows:

   Inventory (or Purchases) 196
      Accounts payable ($200 × 98%)............... 196

b.   Transportation charges paid on goods purchased constitute a part of the cost of those goods (under the cost principle). Transportation charges paid often are recorded in the same account as the purchase cost or in a separate account as follows:

   Transporation in   12
        Cash   12

In this case, the transportation amount for the period usually is added to cost of goods sold on the income statement.

4.   When the periodic inventory system is used, purchase returns are credited to a special account— Purchases returns and allowances. When the perpetual inventory system is used, the Merchandise inventory account is credited.

5.   Selling expenses include such items as freight out, sales salaries, sales commissions, advertising, promotions, sales travel expenses, and depreciation on sales equipment. Selling expenses do not include cost of goods sold. Selling expenses are recorded in the same manner as other operating expenses with appropriate expense account titles.

6—Questions for Self Evaluation

These questions follow the sequence of the discussions in the chapter. However, they do not cover all of the points discussed in the chapter. After studying the chapter, try to answer each question to the best of your ability without referring again to the chapter. After answering all of them, turn to the solutions in the back and evaluate yourself. This should provide a valuable guide for deciding how much additional study you should commit to the chapter.

1. Under the revenue principle, sales revenue is recognized when the (a) _____
   and the amount recognized is the (b) _____.

2. Service revenue is recognized when the service job finally is paid for. _____ T; _____ F

3. Sales revenue minus cost of goods sold equals _____.

4. Gross sales revenue minus sales returns and allowances equals _____.

5. Company X reported the following amounts: Gross margin, $30,000; Sales returns and allowances, $3,000; and Gross sales revenue, $80,000. Therefore, cost of goods sold was $ _____.

6. Company Z reported the following: Sales revenue, $50,000 and gross margin, 60 percent of sales revenue. Therefore, cost of goods sold was $ _____.

7. Explain what is meant by credit terms, 3/10, n/30.

   _____

   _____

8. Assume sales of $16,000 of which 1/4 was on credit. Give the journal entries to:

   (a) Record the sale.

   _____ _____ _____

   _____ _____ _____

   _____ _____ _____

   _____ _____ _____

   (b) Record the credit collection.

   _____ _____ _____

   _____ _____ _____

   _____ _____ _____

9. Assume a credit sale was made on January 10, 19B, with an invoice price of $400; terms were 2/10, n/30. Give the journal entries to:

    (a) Record the sale (use the net method).

       _____ _____ _____

       _____ _____ _____

       _____ _____ _____

    (b) Record the collection, assuming collection on January 15, 19B.

       _____ _____ _____

       _____ _____ _____

       _____ _____ _____

    (c) Record the collection, assuming instead that collection was on January 25, 19B.

       _____ _____ _____

       _____ _____ _____

       _____ _____ _____

       _____ _____ _____

10. Sales revenue is the cash equivalent received (or to be received) including all financing charges if on credit. _____ T; _____ F

11. Cash discounts and trade discounts mean the same thing. _____ T; _____ F

12. Bad debt expense on credit sales must be recorded as an estimate at the end of each accounting period under the matching principle because _____

_____

_____

_____

_____

_____

13. The contra account to the account receivable account usually is titled _____.

14. Company M reported the following **current** assets: Cash, $15,000; Accounts receivable, $30,000, Merchandise inventory, $35,000, Prepaid insurance, $1,200; and Allowance for doubtful accounts, $1,500. Therefore, total current assets was:

    A. $81,200
    B. $84,200
    C. $82,700
    D. $80,300
    E. None of the above; it was $_____.

15. Assume a $200 account receivable was recorded during 19A because of a sale on credit to J. Doe. At the end of 19D, it was determined that this amount would never be collected. At December 31, 19D, it is written off by crediting accounts receivable and debiting bad debt expense.

    (a) Did this violate one of the fundamental accounting principles? Yes _____. No _____.

    (b) If yes, which one? _____ .

16. During 19D, X Retailers recorded sales revenues of $60,000 of which $20,000 was on credit. The company has experienced a bad debt loss rate of 1¼ percent of credit sales.

    (a) Give the adjusting entry at December 31, 19D, to record bad dept expense.

    _____ _____ _____

    _____ _____ _____

    _____ _____ _____

    (b) A 19D account receivable from J. Doe amounting to $100 is to be written off as uncollectible on June 30, 19E. Give the required entry in 19E. If none is required explain why.

    _____ _____ _____

    _____ _____ _____

    _____ _____ _____

17. An account receivable of $400 has been determined to be uncollectible; hence it is to be written off. Complete the following tabulation:

	Balance	
	Before Write-Off	After Write-Off
Balance sheet:		
(a) Accounts receivable	$9,500	$ _____
(b) Allowance for doubtful accounts	1,000	_____
(c) Estimated realizable value (net accounts receivable)	_____	_____
Income statement:		
(d) Bad debt expense..........................	$ 350	_____

18. The balance of the Allowance for doubtful accounts, after the bad debt adjusting entry at the end of the accounting period, always is the same amount as the balance of bad debt expense for that year (before closing entries). _____ T; _____ F

19. Bad debt expense is not a contra account to Accounts receivable. _____ T; _____ F

20. Company T reported the following amounts: Goods available for sale, $80,000; beginning inventory, $20,000; and ending inventory, 30 percent less than the beginning inventory. Therefore, (a) purchases was $ _____ , and (b) cost of goods sold was $ _____ .

21. When the ending inventory is determined on the basis of an actual physical account, the system used is called the _____ ; in contrast when detailed inventory records are maintained which provide the ending inventory, the system used is called the _____ .

22. The perpetual, but not the periodic, inventory system records provide both the amounts for cost of goods sold and ending inventory. _____ T; _____ F

23. Purchases of merchandise for resale are debited to the "Purchases" account for both the periodic and perpetual inventory systems. _____ T; _____ F

24. A sale of merchandise for cash requires only one entry under the periodic inventory system and two entries under the perpetual inventory system. _____ T; _____ F

25. A purchase of merchandise (for resale) for cash requires only one entry under either the periodic or the perpetual inventory system. _____ T; _____ F

26. Complete the following inventory model:

$$\underline{\hspace{2cm}} + \underline{\hspace{2cm}} - \underline{\hspace{2cm}} = CGS$$

27. Company W purchased merchandise for resale at a cost of $5,000, of which 1/5 was on credit terms 3/5, n/60. Give the journal entry:

(a) To record the purchase (assume a periodic inventory system).

_____   _____   _____
_____   _____   _____
_____   _____   _____
_____   _____   _____

(b) To record payment of the credit amount within five days.

_____   _____   _____
_____   _____   _____
_____   _____   _____
_____   _____   _____

(c) To record payment of the credit amount on day 30 after the purchase.

_____   _____   _____
_____   _____   _____
_____   _____   _____
_____   _____   _____

28. Give the journal entries required for each of the four following transactions of Company Q, assuming: (a) a periodic inventory system is used and (b) a perpetual inventory system is used:

Accounts	(a) Periodic Debit	(a) Periodic Credit	(b) Perpetual Debit	(b) Perpetual Credit
(1) Purchased merchandise, $30,000 cash:				
(2) Sold merchandise, one half of the above purchase for $35,000 cash:				
(3) Returned 1/20 of the merchandise purchased in (1) above because damaged when received; received cash refund				
(4) Customers returned 2 percent of the merchandise sold in (2) above because unsatisfactory (but not damaged). Cash refunds were paid to them.				

29. Throughout the period the Merchandise inventory account balance remains unchanged when the perpetual inventory system is used but does change throughout the period when the periodic inventory system is used. _____ T; _____ F

67

30. When a perpetual inventory system is used, the trial balance before the adjusting entries will show the _____ inventory amount. In contrast, when a periodic inventory system is used, the _____ inventory amount will be shown.

31. Dawson Company uses the perpetual inventory system. As a check a physical inventory of merchandise Item A was taken. It showed 132 units on hand (cost $12 per unit). The perpetual inventory record showed 135 units on hand. Give the indicated entry on the date of the physical count.

_____   _____   _____

_____   _____   _____

_____   _____   _____

32. At the end of the annual accounting period (December 31, 19E), the following data were available:

Beginning merchandise inventory	$10,000	
Purchases of merchandise during the period	70,000	$80,000
Ending merchandise inventory		15,000
Cost of goods sold		$65,000

(a) Give the adjusting and closing entries at December 31, 19E, assuming a periodic inventory system (use Income summary account).

_____   _____   _____

_____   _____   _____

_____   _____   _____

_____   _____   _____

_____   _____   _____

_____   _____   _____

_____   _____   _____

_____   _____   _____

_____   _____   _____

_____   _____   _____

_____   _____   _____

_____   _____   _____

(b) Alternatively, give the adjusting and closing entries at December 31, 19E, assuming a perpetual inventory system (use Income summary account).

_____   _____   _____

_____   _____   _____

_____   _____   _____

_____   _____   _____

_____   _____   _____

33. Match each of the following accounting terms with its proper definition by inserting the letter which identifies the definition in the space next to the term.

Accounting Terms

_____ (1) Aging accounts receivable

_____ (2) Bad debt allowance method

_____ (3) Bad debt loss

_____ (4) Gross margin on sales

_____ (5) Gross method to record revenue

_____ (6) Inventory shrinkage

_____ (7) Markup

_____ (8) Net method to record revenue

_____ (9) Periodic inventory system

_____ (10) Perpetual inventory system

_____ (11) Physical inventory count

_____ (12) Purchase discount

_____ (13) Purchase returns and allowances

_____ (14) Sales discount

_____ (15) Sales returns and allowances

_____ (16) Subsidiary ledgers

_____ (17) Trade discount

Definitions

A. A contra revenue account which is associated with unsatisfactory goods

B. Missing inventory caused by theft, breakage, spoilage and incorrect measurements

C. Actual count of units in inventory

D. Sales revenue is recorded after deducting the amount of the authorized cash discount

E. Sales revenue is recorded without deducting the authorized cash discount

F. A discount that is deducted from list price to arrive at the actual sales price

G. Expense associated with estimated uncollectible accounts receivable

H. Ending inventory and cost of goods sold are determined at the end of the accounting period

I. A group of subaccounts that provides more detail than the general ledger control account

J. A deduction from the cost of purchases associated with unsatisfactory goods

K. The difference between net sales revenue and cost of goods sold

L. Method which bases bad debt expense on an estimate of uncollectible accounts

M. Cash discount offered to encourage prompt payment of account receivable

N. Method to estimate uncollectible accounts based on the age of each account receivable

O. Cash discount received for prompt payment of account payable

P. As a dollar amount, net sales minus cost of goods sold; as a ratio, gross margin divided by net sales revenue

Q. A detailed daily inventory record is maintained continuously during the accounting period

7

Costing Methods for Measuring Inventory and Cost of Goods Sold

PURPOSE OF THIS CHAPTER

Chapter 6 discussed accounting for sales revenue and cost of goods sold. You were introduced to the periodic and perpetual inventory systems. In Chapter 6, we assumed that the cost of items purchased for inventory did not change over time. In reality, however, the unit cost of inventory items often will change each time a new purchase order is placed. In this chapter, we will discuss accounting for inventory and cost of goods sold when unit costs are changing.

HOW TO STUDY THIS CHAPTER

This chapter continues the discussions of cost of goods sold and inventories initiated in Chapter 6. Correct measurement of these two amounts is important because they directly affect the amount of income reported on the income statement and the asset inventory on the balance sheet. The entire chapter should be read carefully, and then you should return to study (a) the effect of inventory errors; (b) the inventory costing methods (FIFO, LIFO, weighted average and specific identification); and (c) the comparative effects of the inventory costing methods on the income statement and balance sheet. The Demonstration Case and the suggested solution merit careful study. After this study respond to the "Questions" to evaluate your understanding of the chapter.

STUDY OUTLINE OF THIS CHAPTER

Part A—Measuring Ending Inventory and Cost of Goods Sold with a Periodic Inventory System

A. Inventories usually are classified as follows:
    Retail or wholesale business:
        Merchandise inventory—goods held for resale to customers.
    Manufacturing business:
        Finished goods inventory—goods manufactured and ready for sale.
        Work in process inventory—goods in the fabrication process but not yet completed.
        Raw materials inventory—items acquired and being held for use in the fabrication process.

B. What items should be included in the ending inventory?

1. The inventory should include all (but only) those goods to which the business has legal ownership at the date of the balance sheet.

    (a) The supplier legally retains ownership to goods on consignment although the goods are in the physical possession of the party that will sell them.

2. Ownership passes from the seller to the purchaser at the time intended by the parties. It usually, but not always, is evidenced by delivery of the goods.

    (a) FOB shipping point—ownership usually passes when the seller delivers the goods to the transportation agent.

    (b) FOB destination—ownership usually passes when the goods are delivered to the buyer at destination.

C. What unit cost should be used in measuring the amount of (a) ending inventory and (b) cost of goods sold for the period?

1. This problem arises when identical items were on hand and/or purchased during the period at different unit costs, some of which remain on hand at the end of the period. Assume the following information for one product (Item A):

	Units	Unit Cost	Total Cost
Beginning inventory	200	$1.00	$200
Purchases during the period	200	1.20	240
Goods available for sale	400		$440
Cost of goods sold	200	?	?
Ending inventory	200	?	?

To prepare an income statement, the total cost of the (a) ending inventory and (b) cost of goods sold must be computed. Should the $1.20 unit cost be assigned to the 200 units sold or to the 200 units remaining in the ending inventory? **This problem involves the assignment of unit costs.**

2. Methods of assigning unit costs.

    (a) Four different costing methods are available to assign unit cost in order to determine the ending inventory and cost of goods sold amounts. The business may select the one it deems appropriate. They are:

        (1) FIFO (i.e., first-in, first-out)
        (2) LIFO (i.e., last-in, first-out)
        (3) Average cost(i.e., weighted average)
        (4) Specific identification

    (b) The results of using each of the first three methods of costing inventory and cost of goods sold, in the illustration given above in D.1, for Item A, are as follows:

Method	Ending Inventory	Cost of Goods Sold

FIFO:
  Ending inventory, newest
    unit cost.................
  Cost of goods sold, oldest
    unit cost.................
	..... 200 units @ $1.20 = $240	..... 200 units @ $1.00 = $200

LIFO:
  Ending inventory, oldest
    unit cost.................
  Cost of goods sold, newest
    unit cost.................
	..... 200 units @ $1.00 = $200	..... 200 units @ $1.20 = $240

Average cost:
  Both the ending inventory
    and cost of goods sold
    costed at the weighted
    average cost of:
    $440 ÷ 400 units = $1.10
  Ending inventory............
  Cost of goods sold..........
	..... 200 units @ $1.10 = $220	..... 200 units @ $1.10 = $220

    (c.) Unit cost is determined in accordance with the cost principle. Therefore, unit cost includes the following:

        1. Cash (or cash equivalent) paid or to be paid.
        2. Less: Any cash discounts specified, whether taken or not. See Chapter 6.
        3. Plus: Any handling costs—freight, insurance during transit, and related storage costs.

3. Because the amount of the ending inventory and the amount of cost of goods sold are different under each of the three costing methods, each will cause a different amount of income and inventory to be reported on the financial statements. No one method can be considered the "best" under all circumstances. A company may elect to use any one for all inventory items, or a different method for different types of items stocked.

4. One of the fundamental accounting principles listed in the textbook is called the comparability principle. If businesses were allowed to change their accounting procedures at will, and for no sound reason, it would be possible to manipulate income and balance sheet amounts in various ways. The comparability principle prevents this kind of "willy-nilly" change. It holds that all accounting concepts, standards, and measurement approaches should be applied in a consistent way from period to period (except when a better method can be justified).

Part B—Application of the Perpetual Inventory System and Selected Inventory Costing Methods

D. Each inventory costing method (see the four methods listed in 2(a) above) may be used with either the periodic or the perpetual inventory system.

1. Illustrations of application of the four inventory costing methods with the (a) periodic inventory system, and (b) perpetual inventory system. Basic illustrative data given in D1 above.

(a) **Periodic Inventory System**—ending inventory determined by physical inventory count to be 200 units of Item A:

Items	FIFO		LIFO		Weighted Average		Specific Identification*	
Sales revenue		$350		$350		$350		$350
CGS:								
BI		200		200		200		200
Pur		240		240		240		240
Gds Avail		440		440		440		440
					($440 ÷ 400 = $1.10)		($1.00 × 150)	
EI(200 Units)	($1.10 × 200)	240	($1.00 × 200)	200	($1.10 × 200)	220	+ ($1.20 × 50)	210
CGS		200		240		220		230
Gross Margin		150		110		130		120
Expenses		100		100		100		100
Pretax income**		$ 50		$ 10		$ 30		$ 20

*Specific identification: Assumed sales, 50 units from the beginning inventory and 150 units from current purchases.

**Observe the significant differences of pretax income among the four costing methods, given exactly the same set of facts otherwise.

(b) **Perpetual Inventory System**—Ending inventory and cost of goods sold provided by detailed perpetual inventory records.

Perpetual Inventory Record—Item A

FIFO:	Purchases			Issues		(CGS)↓	Balance		
	Units	Unit Cost	Total Cost	Units	Unit Cost	Total Cost	Units	Unit Cost	Total Cost
Beginning Inventory							200	1.00	200
Purchases	200	1.20	240				{ 200 200	1.00 1.20	200 240
Sale				200	1.00	200	200	1.20	240-EI

LIFO:									
Beginning Inventory							200	1.00	200
Purchases	200	1.20	240				{ 200 200	1.00 1.20	200 240
Sale				200	1.20	240	200	1.00	200-EI

Moving Average:									
Beginning Inventory							200	1.00	200
Purchases	200	1.20	240				400	1.10	440
Sale				200	1.10	220	200	1.10	220-EI

Specific Identification:									
Beginning Inventory							200	1.00	200
Purchases	200	1.20	240				{ 200 200	1.00 1.20	200 240
Sale				{ 50 150	1.00 1.20	50 180	150 50	1.00 1.20	150 } EI 60 }

For Income Statement:
Cost of goods sold ⟶

For Balance Sheet:
Merchandise inventory ⟶

76

E. Other inventory considerations.

1. When any of the merchandise in inventory is damaged, obsolete, or shop-worn, it should not be valued in the ending inventory at original purchase cost but at the present net realizable value (when that is below cost). Net realizable value is the expected net amount to be realized when the merchandise finally is sold. For example, assume that an item that cost $50 when it was purchased is damaged so that it can be sold for only $20 net (i.e., net of any renovation costs incurred and any selling expenses which would be incurred). It should be costed in the inventory at the lower amount, $20 per unit.

2. In certain situations, a rule is applied to items in the ending inventory, called the **lower-of-cost-or-market rule** (LCM). It is applied when an item in inventory can be replaced (i.e., purchased) at the inventory date at a cost less than the amount paid for the item when it originally was purchased.

   (a) Assume five units of an item that cost $10 per unit are included in the ending inventory. Because of a drop in the market they now can be purchased for $9 per unit. The latter unit amount should be used in computing the amount of the ending inventory for this item (i.e., the ending inventory for this item would be: 45 × $9 = $45).

3. Estimating ending inventory and cost of goods sold. The gross margin ratio (gross margin divided by net sales revenue) can be used to estimate inventory and cost of goods sold. This method is useful when the periodic inventory system is used and monthly or quarterly financial statements must be prepared. This procedure is illustrated in the text for Patz Company.

4. The ending inventory of one period is the beginning inventory of the next period; therefore, the ending inventory amount affects the (a) income statements of two consecutive periods, (b) inventory on the balance sheet, and (c) owners' equity.

(a) If the ending inventory is **overstated**:

  (1) On the income statement: Cost of goods sold will be understated, and pretax income will be overstated.

  (2) On the balance sheet: Inventory and owners' equity (retained earnings) will be overstated.

(b) If the ending inventory is **understated**:

  (1) On the income statement: Cost of goods sold will be overstated and pretax income will be understated.

  (2) On the balance sheet: Inventory and retained earnings will be understated.

(c) Two important facts about inventories:

  (1) The ending inventory for one period is the beginning inventory for the next period.

  (2) The beginning and ending inventories have opposite effects on pretax income.

(d) An error in the ending inventory of one period will cause an error of the same amount, and in the same direction, in pretax income. That error is carried over to the next period in the beginning inventory where it will have an opposite effect on pretax income. As a consequence, an inventory error in one period will cause (1) the pretax income for each of two consecutive periods to be incorrect by the same amount, but in opposite directions; and (2) the incorrect pretax income amounts for the two consecutive periods to sum to the correct total pretax income for the two periods combined.

7—Questions for Self Evaluation

These questions follow the sequence of the discussions in the chapter. However, they do not cover all of the points discussed in the chapter. After studying the chapter, try to answer each question to the best of your ability without referring again to the chapter. After answering all of them, turn to the solutions in the back and evaluate yourself. This should provide a valuable guide for deciding how much additional study you should commit to the chapter.

1. Match the following:

   (1) _____ Items acquired for processing into completed products   A. Finished goods inventory

   (2) _____ Goods being fabricated but not finished   B. Merchandise inventory

   (3) _____ Goods held for resale; purchased in state ready for sale   C. Work in process inventory

   (4) _____ Goods manufactured by the business for sale   D. Raw materials inventory

2. What is the general rule for determining what goods should be included in the ending inventory?

   _____

   _____

3. When does the buyer or the seller own goods during transit? If shipped FOB destination, goods are

   owned by the _____; if shipped FOB shipping point, goods are owned by the

   _____.

4. Who should include in its inventory any goods held on consignment? The consignor _____ or the

   consignee _____ ?

5. At the end of 19A, Company X had goods (cost $10,000) out on consignment to Company Y.

   A. Company X should include the goods in inventory.
   B. Company Y should include the goods in inventory.
   C. Both companies should include the goods in inventory.
   D. Neither company should include the goods in inventory.
   E. None of the above.

6. Unit cost is determined in accordance with the _____ principle.

7. On December 23, 19A, Small Stereo Company purchased on credit ten portable FM/AM cassette radios for resale. The invoice price was $50, subject to terms 2/10, n/30. Small paid the freight bill amounting to $4. The liability will be paid January 15, 19B. The unit cost that should be used for the

   19A ending inventory (two on hand) should be $ _____.

8. Match the following:

   (1) _____ Periodic inventory system   A. BI + P − EI = CGS

   (2) _____ Perpetual inventory system   B. BI + P − CGS = EI

9. The perpetual inventory system accomplishes the objective of measuring cost of goods sold and the inventory amount on a current basis by means of _____ _____ .

In contrast, the periodic inventory system does this on an end-of-the-period basis by means of ___ _____ .

10. The four inventory costing methods (FIFO, LIFO, Weighted Average, and Specific Identification) usually will produce (assume 4 percent inflation):

   A. About the same pretax income for the period.
   B. Significantly different pretax income for the period.
   C. No effect on the reported pretax income of the following accounting period.
   D. No material effect on the inventory amount of the periods balance sheet.
   E. None of the above is reasonably correct.

11. Of the four inventory costing methods, which one is the most subject to manipulation? _____ .

12. FIFO assigns the _____ unit costs to cost of goods sold; whereas LIFO assigns the _____ unit costs to cost of goods sold.

13. LIFO assigns the _____ unit costs to inventory; whereas FIFO assigns the _____ unit costs to inventory.

14. In applying a moving weighted average, a new average unit cost is computed after each _____ .

15. How does federal income taxation affect a company's decision to select LIFO rather than FIFO when costs are rising?

_____

_____

16. Match the following:

   (1) _____ Emphasizes the balance sheet   A.   LIFO

   (2) _____ Emphasizes the income statement   B.   FIFO

17. The following data on Product B are available in respect to goods available for sale:

	Units	Unit Cost
Beginning inventory................	100	$5
Purchase No. 1	200	6
Purchase No. 2	100	7
Total—goods available for sale	400	

Complete the following assuming 300 units were sold (assume periodic inventory system):

		Cost Apportionment	
Inventory Costing Method		Cost of Goods Sold	Ending Inventory
(a) Example—specific identification		$1,710	$690
(b) Average (weighted).........................		_____	_____
(c) FIFO		_____	_____
(d) LIFO		_____	_____

18. The ending inventory is to be estimated on the basis of the data given below. You are to fill in the blanks.

Recent gross margin ratio, 42%
Sales revenue $100,000
Beginning inventory .... $ 15,000
Purchases 55,000
Goods available for sale.............. $ 70,000

(a) Ending inventory .... _____

(b) Cost of goods sold .... _____

(c) Gross margin on sales .... _____

19. Indicate with a check mark the inventory costing method usually used with (a) perpetual and (b) periodic inventory systems.

		Usually Used With—	
Inventory Costing Method		Perpetual Inventory	Periodic Inventory
(a) Weighted average (annual average)		_____	_____
(b) Moving average		_____	_____
(c) Specific identification		_____	_____
(d) FIFO		_____	_____
(e) LIFO priced at the end of the period		_____	_____
(f) LIFO priced currently (during the period)		_____	_____

20. Tye company sells major household appliances on credit. Occasionally, an appliance must be repossessed because of nonpayment. Repossessed appliances are recorded as "Inventory of Used Appliances" at their net realizable value. On March 1, 19E, a refrigerator was repossessed which was sold new for $800 (original cost new, $410). The unpaid balance at date of repossession was $245. The company estimated that it would cost $50 to ready it for resale (as used) for $300. The cost to resell will be approximately $30. At date of repossession, and after the estimates were made, the inventory account for this used item should be debited in the amount of:

A. $410   E. $380
B. $300   F. $220
C. $350   G. None of the above, it
D. $250   would be $ _____ .

Complete the journal entry given below to record the repossession.

Inventory of used appliances . . . . _____

Allowance for doubtful accounts (or loss
on repossession) . . . . _____

Accounts receivable . . . . _____

21. Inventory items that are damaged, obsolete, or shopworn should be measured and reported at _____ rather than at cost.

22. If an inventory item cost $90 when purchased, and at the end of the period it can be purchased in the market for $80, it should be included in the ending inventory at $ _____ under the _____ rule.

23. The _____ principle holds that in accounting all concepts, principles, and measurement approaches should be applied on a consistent basis and in a similar way from one period to the next to assure comparable financial reports.

24. Nekir Company purchases store supplies (not for resale) in advance of use. The supplies are kept in a storeroom pending usage as needed. At the start of the period the Store supplies inventory account showed a debit balance of $400.

   (a) During the period store supplies were purchased for cash at a cost of $900. Give the journal entry.

   _____ _____ _____

   _____ _____ _____

   _____ _____ _____

   (b) At the end of the period, an inventory of store supplies showed $325 to be on hand. Give the adjusting journal entry.

   _____ _____ _____

   _____ _____ _____

   _____ _____ _____

25. The ending inventory for 19A will affect both the 19A and 19B income statements but not the 19B balance sheet. _____ T; _____ F

26. An understatement of the 19B ending inventory will overstate 19B income and not affect 19C income.

   _____ T; _____ F

27. There is a direct relationship between errors in the ending inventory and pretax income in any given year, and an inverse relationship between errors in the beginning inventory and pretax income in any given year.

   _____ T; _____ F

28. Company X reported pretax incomes as follows: 19A—$8,000; 19B—$6,000. It now has been determined that the ending inventory for 19A was overstated by $1,100. The correct pretax income is:

19A: $ _____

19B: $ _____

29. Company Z reported pretax incomes as follows: 19A—$20,000 and 19B—$30,000. Later two errors were discovered, the ending inventory for 19A was understated by $5,000, and the ending inventory for 19B also was understated by $1,000. The correct pretax incomes are:

A. 19A—$25,000; 19B—$31,000
B. 19A—$15,000; 19B—$29,000
C. 19A—$25,000; 19B—$26,000
D. 19A—$15,000; 19B—$34,000
E. None of the above; it was: 19A, $ _____ ; 19B, $ _____ .

30. Match each of the following accounting terms with its proper definition by inserting the letter which identifies the definition in the space next to the term.

Accounting Terms

_____ (1) Comparability principle

_____ (2) Consignments

_____ (3) Finished goods inventory

_____ (4) First-in, first-out

_____ (5) Gross margin method

_____ (6) Last-in, first-out

_____ (7) Lower of cost or market

_____ (8) Merchandise inventory

_____ (9) Moving weighted average

_____ (10) Net realizable value

_____ (11) Periodic inventory system

_____ (12) Perpetual inventory system

_____ (13) Raw materials inventory

_____ (14) Specific identification

_____ (15) Weighted average

_____ (16) Work in process inventory

Definitions

A. Goods in the process of being manufactured that are not yet complete

B. Inventory costing method that assumes the oldest units are the first units sold

C. A detailed daily inventory record is updated continuously during the accounting period

D. Accounting methods should be consistently applied from one period to the next

E. Items acquired for the purpose of processing into finished goods

F. Inventory costing method that assumes the newest units are the first units sold

G. Ending inventory and cost of goods sold are determined at the end of the accounting period

H. Method to estimate ending inventory based on the gross margin ratio

I. Estimated amount to be realized when goods are sold, less disposal costs

J. Inventory costing method that identifies the cost of the specific item that was sold

K. Goods held for resale in the ordinary course of business

L. Inventory costing method that averages all purchase costs to calculate a weighted average unit cost; used with periodic inventory system

M. Weighted average inventory costing method applied to the perpetual inventory system

N. Goods in possession of a seller but legal title is retained by the supplier

O. Departure from cost principle which serves to recognize a "holding" loss when replacement cost drops below cost

P. Manufactured goods which are completed and ready for sale

Cash, Short-Term Investments in Securities and Receivables

PURPOSE OF THIS CHAPTER

The discussions in the two preceding chapters have focused primarily on the income statement. In this chapter, the focus will shift to the balance sheet. Our discussion of balance sheet classifications will begin with the most liquid (or current) assets: cash, short-term investments, and receivables. In the previous chapter, we discussed accounting for another important current asset, inventories.

HOW TO STUDY THIS CHAPTER

This chapter discusses three topics: (a) cash, (b) short-term investments, and (c) receivables. Although this chapter is not difficult, you should study each part carefully as a separate unit. The Demonstration Case and the suggested solution will add considerably to your knowledge of notes payable as well as notes receivable.

STUDY OUTLINE OF THIS CHAPTER

Part A—Safeguarding and Reporting Cash

A.   Cash is the most liquid of the assets. Cash includes money and instruments, such as a check, money order, or bank draft, which banks normally accept for deposit and immediate credit to the depositor's account.

1.   Cash is the sum of the cash on hand, cash deposited in the bank, and petty cash.

2.   Because cash is the asset most vulnerable to theft and fraud, strict control procedures should be used. These procedures are called an **internal control system** for cash. The procedures include:

(a)   Complete separation of the jobs of receiving cash from disbursing cash.
(b)   Complete separation of the procedures of accounting for cash receipts and cash disbursements.
(c)   Complete separation of the physical handling of cash from all phases of the accounting functions.
(d)   Require that all cash receipts be deposited in a bank each day.
(e)   Require that all cash payments be made by prenumbered checks. Require separate approval of the expenditure and of the preparation of the check.
(f)   Assign the cash payment approval and check signing responsibilities to different individuals.

B. All companies maintain one or more bank accounts.

1. At the end of each month the bank statement should be **reconciled** with the cash records of the company. This reconciliation has four purposes:

(a) To determine whether errors have been made either by the bank or by the company.
(b) To provide data for journal entries to be made in the accounts of the company for certain items on the bank statement such as bank service charges.
(c) To determine the outstanding checks—checks written by the company that have not yet been cashed by the holder.
(d) To develop the correct cash balance that is reported on the balance sheet at the end of the period. The correct cash balance must include the correct cash balance in the bank plus all cash on hand (i.e., undeposited cash including any petty cash).

2. You should study the bank reconciliation illustrated in the textbook (Exhibit 8-3); including the (a) cash account, (b) bank statement, and (c) resulting accounting entries. Especially note the following:

(a) The bank reconciliation starts with the **ending** book and bank balances (not the beginning balances).
(b) The depositor's ending book balance is increased and decreased on the bank reconciliation for all amounts reflected on the bank statement that have not been recorded already in the depositor's cash account (e.g., four items in Exhibit 8-3).
(c) The bank statement ending balance is increased for all cash items (debits) that have been recorded already by the depositor but have not been included in the bank statement balance (e.g., deposits in transit and cash on hand in Exhibit 8-3). The ending bank balance is decreased by the items (credits) that already have been recorded by the depositor but have not been deducted from the bank statement (e.g., outstanding checks).
(d) Journal entries must be made for all additions and deductions to the "Depositor's Books" to bring the Depositor's Cash Account to the correct cash balance. Observe in Exhibit 8-3 in the textbook that there were four such items; therefore, four journal entries are shown in Exhibit 8-4.

C. Cash shortages and cash overages during the period are recorded in an account usually called "Cash Over and Short." At the end of the accounting period a debit balance in this account is reported as an expense and a credit balance as a miscellaneous revenue.

Part B—Measuring and Reporting Short-Term Investments

D. Many companies have extra cash in addition to the minimum required for normal transactions. Often they purchase stocks, bonds, or certificates of deposit (CDs), as short-term investments in order to earn a return on the otherwise idle cash.

   1. Short-term investments are classified as current assets on the balance sheet because they meet a twofold test of: (1) marketability (can be sold readily), and (2) a short-term holding period (the intention of management is to convert them to cash during the current or upcoming year).

   2. Investments that do not meet the twofold test must be reported as a noncurrent asset under the balance sheet caption, "Investments and Funds."

E. Short-term investments are accounted for at their cash equivalent cost (when acquired) in conformity with the cost principle.

   1. W Corporation purchased 100 shares of the capital stock of X Corporation, for cash at $25 per share, as a short-term investment. The journal entry by W Corporation is:

      Short-term investments 2,500
            Cash   2,500

2. A few months later a cash dividend of $2 per share on the X Corportion stock is received by W Corporation. The dividend is recorded by W Corporation as follows:

Cash 200
    Investment revenue 200

3. Short-term investments, after acquisition, are reported at lower-of-cost-or-market (LCM) similar to merchandise inventory. Assume it is at the end of the year and the stock of X Company is selling for $22 per share. The following adjusting entry is made by W Corporation at year end:

Unrealized loss on short-term investments
  ($25 − $22) × 100............................ 300
    Allowance to reduce ST investments to market   300

The contra account, Allowance to reduce ST investments to market is reported on the balance sheet as a deduction from the balance in the account "Short-Term Investments."

4. If in a subsequent period (i.e., prior to their sale) the market price increases, the investments would be written up but not in excess of their original cost. Assume in a subsequent accounting period, the price of X company stock increased to $26 per share. The journal entry is:

Allowance to reduce ST investments to market .. 300
    Unrealized loss recovery on ST investments   300

5. LCM is applied on a portfolio basis, not to each individual security in the portfolio.

Part C—Measuring and Reporting Receivables

F. Short-term (i.e., current assets) receivables usually are comprised of three types: trade receivables, special receivables, and short-term notes receivable.

1. Trade accounts receivable are amounts due from regular customers for goods sold to them; they usually are called "Accounts Receivable."

2. Special accounts receivable are the nontrade receivables.

3. Short-term notes receivable. Notes receivable differ from trade and special receivables because, instead of being "open" accounts, they are represented by a formal document—a note. Notes receivable may be either trade or nontrade.

G. Trade accounts receivable—These receivables result from the sale of merchandise to customers and should be recorded net of any cash discounts (whether taken or not).

1. Accounts receivable are reported on the balance sheet at their net realizable value (i.e., after deduction of the contra account "Allowance for doubtful accounts").

2. Review the discussion of accounts receivable in Chapter 6 in this Study Guide and in the textbook.

H. Special accounts receivable arise from nontrade transactions, such as the sale of an operational asset or investment on short-term credit.

I. Notes receivable—A note is a written promise to pay a specified amount of cash at a specified date in the future. There are two parties to a note: the **maker**, who owes the debt; and the **payee**, to whom the debt is owed. The payee views a note as a note receivable; the maker views it as a note payable.

1. In business, people never loan money without interest (a cost representing the time value of money), therefore all commercial notes involve interest. A note involves two distinctly different amounts: (a) principal (the amount loaned) and (b) interest (the amount charged for use of the principal loaned).

(a) Notes may be either interest bearing or noninterest bearing. An **interest-bearing note** specifies the rate of interest on the note. In addition to the principal, interest is payable at the maturity date of the note (or sometimes at specified dates during the term of the note). In contrast, a **noninterest-bearing note** usually specifies no interest rate. The interest is taken out of the cash proceeds when the note is signed. At maturity date, only the face amount of the note is paid.

2. Interest on a note is calculated as follows:

Principal $\times$ Annual rate of interest $\times$ Fraction of year $=$ Interest amount

Example: A $1,000, 12 percent interest-bearing note, due in 4 months:

$$\$1,000 \times 12\% \times 4/12 = \$40 \text{ interest}$$

3. Journal entries to record an interest-bearing note—A $1,000 interest-bearing note (12%) was received by W Company for goods sold to a customer. The sale is recorded by W Company as follows:

Notes receivable	1,000	
Sales revenue		1,000

Collection of the note, plus interest, 120 days later is recorded as follows:

Cash ($1,000 + $40)	1,040	
Notes receivable		1,000
Interest revenue		40

J. Discounting a note receivable—A business that has a current cash need may have a note receivable that is due several months in the future. As a consequence, it may decide to sell (or discount) the note to a bank. In this case the business (payee) receives cash, and the maker of the note will pay the bank at maturity date (the principal of the note plus interest). The bank, of course, enters into such transactions in order to earn interest revenue. Often the bank will charge a higher rate of interest than is called for on the note; the person or business discounting the note must pay the interest difference.

1. T Company has a $3,000, one-year note receivable with an annual interest rate of 12 percent. At maturity, the principal, plus 12 percent interest, will be collected. After holding the note receivable for three months, the business discounts it to the bank at a 15 percent rate and receives cash. The note is endorsed and turned over to the bank.

   (a) The cash received by T Company from the bank is computed as follows:

Principal amount	$3,000.00
Add: Interest due at maturity ($3,000 × 12%)	360.00
Total maturity value—amount subject to discount	$3,360.00
Discount—interest charged by the bank: $3,360 × 15% × 9/12 =	378.00
Proceeds—amount the bank pays for the note	$2,982.00

   (b) The discounting of the above note requires the following journal entry:

Cash (the proceeds computed above)	2,982	
Interest expense (the difference)*	18	
Note receivable (the principal)		3,000

   *This is the net amount of interest T Company paid.

2. Notes usually are **negotiable**, which means that they can be transferred by the holder to someone else by endorsement.

8—Questions for Self Evaluation

These questions follow the sequence of the discussions in the chapter. However, they do not cover all of the points discussed in the chapter. After studying the chapter, try to answer each question to the best of your ability without referring again to the chapter. After answering all of them, turn to the solutions in the back and evaluate yourself. This should provide a valuable guide for deciding how much additional study you should commit to the chapter.

1. Cash is the most _____ of all assets.

2. Indicate the composition of cash by entering one check mark on each line under the appropriate column to the right.

| | | Cash Usually Should— | |
Item		Include	Exclude
(a) Currency		_____	_____
(b) Postage stamps		_____	_____
(c) Checks from others (collectible)		_____	_____
(d) Notes receivable (short term)		_____	_____
(e) Bank drafts		_____	_____
(f) Postdated checks received from customers		_____	_____
(g) Money orders		_____	_____
(h) Cash in a closed bank (collection doubtful)		_____	_____
(i) IOUs		_____	_____
(j) Deposit in the bank		_____	_____
(k) Cash on hand (for change)		_____	_____
(l) Any instrument that the bank will accept for immediate deposit		_____	_____

3. Cash and short-term investments are classified as current assets because they are cash, or will be converted into cash to pay liabilities during the _____ or during the _____ whichever is the longer.

4. _____ refers to those policies and procedures of the entity designed to safeguard the assets.

5. The two functions of cash handling and accounting for cash should be assigned to different individuals in order to (a) _____

   (b) _____ .

6. A basic guideline in the internal control of cash is to: (a) _____ all cash receipts, and (b) _____ by check.

7. Each month the bank provides the depositor with a bank statement which includes the following:

(a) _____

(b) _____

(c) _____

(d) _____

(e) A listing of any bank charges (service charges) and credits, made by the bank to the depositor's account.

8. A general internal control rule is that all cash payments should be made by check. However, it is often advisable to establish a small _____ from which small cash payments are made for incidental items.

9. What is a compensating balance? _____

_____

_____

_____

_____

10. A bank reconciliation results in a reconciliation (a check) of the beginning (of the current period) book and bank balances. _____ T; _____ F

11. In a bank reconciliation, outstanding checks are deducted from, and deposits in transit are added to the "balance per bank statement." _____ T; _____ F

12. At the end of March the Cash account on the depositor's books showed the following:

Cash			No. 101
March 1 balance	5,000	March checks	19,500
March deposits	20,000		

The bank statement received at the end of March showed the following:

March 1, balance	$ 5,000
Deposits..	18,000
Note collected for depositor (principal, $300 plus interest, $24)	324
Checks cashed	(16,000)
Bank service charge	(15)
March 31, balance	$ 7,309

Assume no outstanding checks or deposits in transit at the end of the prior month.

94

(a) Complete the following reconciliation for March:

Depositor's Book		Bank Statement	
Balance .... $ _____		Balance .... $ _____	
Additions:		Additions:	
_____	_____	_____	_____
_____	_____	_____	_____
Deductions:		Deductions:	
_____	_____	_____	_____
_____	_____	_____	_____
Correct cash balance .... $ _____		Correct cash balance .... $ _____	

(b) The above reconciliation requires two journal entries by the depositor. They are:

(1) _____ _____ _____

_____ _____ _____

_____ _____ _____

_____ _____ _____

(2) _____ _____ _____

_____ _____ _____

_____ _____ _____

_____ _____ _____

13. To be classified as a current asset, a short-term investment must meet the twofold test of

(a) _____ and

(b) _____ .

14. Short-term investments are reported on the balance sheet as an asset under the caption:

_____ . Long-term investments are reported under the caption:

_____ .

15. X Company owns 100 shares of the capital stock of Y Company. When purchased on January 30, 19A, the shares cost $2,000. At December 31, 19A, the end of the annual accounting period, the market value was $2,300. Show how this short-term investment should be reported on the balance sheet at December 31, 19A.

_____

_____

_____

16. The lower-of-cost-or-market rule violates both the cost principle and the comparability principle because of the _____ principle.

17. Give the journal entry for Company A for each of the following cash transactions:

(a) Purchased, as a short-term investment, 500 shares of the capital stock of Company B. Cost $5,000 plus $200 fees and transfer costs.

_____   _____   _____
_____   _____   _____
_____   _____   _____
_____   _____   _____

(b) Collected dividends of $1.50 per share.

_____   _____   _____
_____   _____   _____
_____   _____   _____

(c) Sold one half of the shares for $2,500.

_____   _____   _____
_____   _____   _____
_____   _____   _____
_____   _____   _____

18. Give the journal entry for Company R for each of the following transactions:

(a) Purchased for cash, 800 shares of the capital stock of Company S for $6,000 plus $400 fees and transfer costs.

_____   _____   _____
_____   _____   _____
_____   _____   _____
_____   _____   _____

(b) Collected cash dividends of $1 per share.

_____   _____   _____
_____   _____   _____
_____   _____   _____
_____   _____   _____

(c) At the end of the accounting period the stock of Company S had a market value of $7.50 per share.

_____   _____   _____
_____   _____   _____
_____   _____   _____
_____   _____   _____

19. A note that is transferable by endorsement is said to be a _____ note.

20. The person who signs a promissory note is known as the (a) _____, and the person to whom payment is to be made is known as the (b) _____.

21. (a) When a note specifies a rate of interest which is to be paid at one or more dates in the future, in addition to the principal amount, it is known as an _____ note.

    (b) When a note does not specify a rate of interest and no interest is to be paid in addition to the face amount of the note, it is known as a _____ note.

22. A noninterest-bearing note does not require the maker to pay interest. _____ T; _____ F

23. A _____ exists when a bank requires the business to maintain a minimum amount in its bank account as a loan condition.

24. Give journal entries for Wilson Company for the following transactions assuming the annual accounting period ends on December 31.

    (a) October 1, 19A—sold merchandise for $600 and received a one-year, 15 percent interest-bearing note receivable for that amount. The interest is payable at the maturity date.

    _____ _____ _____
    _____ _____ _____
    _____ _____ _____
    _____ _____ _____

    (b) December 31, 19A—adjusting entry for accrued interest.

    _____ _____ _____
    _____ _____ _____
    _____ _____ _____
    _____ _____ _____

    (c) Collected the note on September 30, 19B (assume no reversing entry on January 1, 19B):

    _____ _____ _____
    _____ _____ _____
    _____ _____ _____
    _____ _____ _____

25. On February 1, 19A, Elvis Company sold merchandise for $2,000 and received a six-month, 15 percent, interest-bearing note for the amount. The company recorded the transaction as follows:

    Notes receivable (trade) 2,000
          Sales revenue   2,000

On April 1, 19A, Elvis Company discounted (sold) the note to the bank at a discount rate of 16 percent. Give the entry to record the transaction and show the computations.

26. Match each of the following accounting terms with its proper definition by inserting the letter which identifies the definition in the space next to the term.

Accounting Terms	Definitions
_____ (1) Bank reconciliation	A. An endorser (on a negotiable instrument) is liable for its payment if the maker defaults; a contingent liability exists for the endorser
_____ (2) Bank statement	
_____ (3) Cash	B. Valuation of an investment at either (a) original cost or (b) current market whichever is lower
_____ (4) Cash over and short	C. Implementation principles may be modified in application for (a) immaterial amounts, (b) conservatism, (c) industry peculiarities
_____ (5) Certificates of deposit	
_____ (6) Compensating balances	D. Checks written by a depositor that have not yet been cleared (cashed) by the depositor's bank
_____ (7) Contingent liability	E. Failure of the maker (payor) of a note to pay it by its maturity date
_____ (8) Default of note receivable	F. Money and any instrument that banks will accept for immediate increase in depositor's checking account
_____ (9) Deposits in transit	G. A group of securities (stock or bonds) held as an investment; grouped to be accounted for as one unit
_____ (10) Discounting a note receivable	H. Deposits made by a depositor that have not yet been reported on the bank statement
_____ (11) Holding (unrealized) loss	I. Usually a formal (written) instrument that specifies the terms of a debt; it is transferable by endorsement
_____ (12) Internal control	J. A small amount of cash set aside for making small cash payments instead of writing checks
_____ (13) Investments portfolio	K. Difference between original purchase cost of the investor and the current market value; if market value is lower there is an unrealized loss (if not sold)
_____ (14) Lower of cost or market	
_____ (15) Negotiable instrument	L. Difference between the amount of cash held at a particular time and the amount the cash records call for
_____ (16) Notes receivable	M. A written promise that requires another party to pay the business under specified conditions (amount, time, interest)
_____ (17) Outstanding checks	
_____ (18) Petty cash	N. A CD; an investment contract that can be purchased from banks: specifies amount, time, and interest rate
_____ (19) Receivables, short term	O. Receivables that arise from transactions other than merchandise and services sold
_____ (20) Short-term investment	P. Another name for accounts receivable; open accounts owed to the business by trade customers
_____ (21) Special receivables	
_____ (22) Trade receivables	Q. Monthly report from a bank that shows deposits recorded, checks cleared, and a running bank balance
	R. Exists when a bank requires that a specified minimum cash balance must be maintained in the depositor's account
	S. Investment that (a) is marketable and (b) will have a short-term holding period.
	T. Policies and procedures of a business designed to safeguard the assets of the business

U. Short-term notes and accounts owed to the business by regular trade customers.

V. Sale of a note receivable to another party prior to its maturity amount

W. Process of verifying the accuracy of both the bank statement and the cash accounts of the business

9

Operational Assets—Property, Plant, and Equipment; Natural Resources; and Intangibles

PURPOSE OF THIS CHAPTER

The operation of a business requires a combination of assets that are classified on a balance sheet as current, investments and funds, operational, and other. The purpose of this chapter is to discuss operational assets. These assets usually are called property, plant, and equipment and intangible assets (and sometimes fixed assets). Operational assets are the noncurrent assets that a business retains more or less permanently (not for sale) to carry on its continuing and ongoing operations. Operational assets include land, buildings, equipment, fixtures, natural resources, and certain intangible assets (such as a patent). Operational assets are important in carrying out the normal profit-making activities of a business.

HOW TO STUDY THIS CHAPTER

This chapter explains how operational assets are measured, recorded, and reported. Basically, there are two classifications of operational assets: tangible assets, and intangible assets. For each classification the discussions explain and illustrate the accounting; (1) at date of acquisition; (2) during the holding period (i.e., the period of use); and (3) at date of disposal. Each of these three phases is quite similar conceptually for each of the classifications of operational assets. The cost and matching principles provide the guidelines for accounting for operational assets. We recommend that you carefully study the illustrations given in the chapter. The Demonstration Case and the suggested solution merit careful study because they tie together the discussions in the chapter.

STUDY OUTLINE OF THIS CHAPTER

Part A—Property, Plant and Equipment Including Depreciation

A. Operational assets (sometimes called fixed assets) are those noncurrent assets that a business retains for long-term use in operating the business. These assets are not held for resale. Operational assets include:

   1. Tangible assets—those operational assets (often called property, plant, and equipment) that have physical substance such as land, buildings, equipment, furniture, and natural resources.
   2. Intangible assets—those operational assets that have no physical substance, such as patents, copyrights, and franchises. Sometimes referred to simply as intangibles.

B. When acquired operational assets are recorded at the cash equivalent outlays made in obtaining them in conformity with the cost principle. Cash equivalent cost includes the purchase price plus all related outlays made to get the operational asset into position and condition for its intended use.

   1. If an operational asset is paid for with noncash items, the current cash equivalent value of those items is recorded as the cost of the asset.
   2. Costs incurred to prepare an operational asset for use are recorded as a part of the cost.
   3. Summary: Acquisition cost = cash paid + market value of any noncash assets given up + title and legal fees + transportation and installation costs paid by the buyer.
   4. Interest paid during the construction period (such as the construction of an office building) is recorded as a part of the cost of that asset.
   5. The cost of financing the purchase of an asset (e.g., interest expense or discounts lost) is not included in the cost of the asset. Financing costs are reported as an expense in the period in which incurred.

C. During the period of use, the cost of an operational asset must be apportioned to expense in such manner as to match its cost with the revenues earned as a result of using the asset. This apportionment is required by the matching principle. This apportionment is referred to as:

   1. Depreciation—when the asset involved is a tangible operational asset, other than a natural resource, such as plant and equipment.
   2. Depletion—when the asset involved is a natural resource, such as a mineral deposit.
   3. Amortization—when the asset involved is intangible in character, such as a patent.

D. Depreciation is recognized only on those operational assets that have a limited life, such as machinery, buildings, and furniture. In contrast, land is not depreciated.

1. GAAP permits the use of several depreciation methods. To be acceptable, a method must be both rational and systematic.

2. The amount of cost to be depreciated is the actual acquisition cost minus the estimated residual value (i.e., the estimated value of the asset at the end of its estimated useful life). For example:

Actual acquisition cost	$3,500
Residual value (estimated)	500
Amount of asset cost to be depreciated	$3,000

3. Depreciation requires that the useful life of the item be estimated, either in years or in a measure of use (such as units of output).

E. Methods of depreciation:

1. Straight-line method—An equal amount is depreciated each accounting period.

Example: Assume the above asset ($3,000 to be depreciated) has an estimated useful life of five years. The annual depreciation entry is:

Depreciation expense ($3,000 ÷ 5 yrs.)	600	
Accumulated depreciation		600

2. Productive-output method—The amount of depreciation each period depends on the amount of use (i.e., the output).

Example: Assume the above asset has an estimated useful life of 6,000 units. The depreciation rate per unit would be: $3,000 ÷ 6,000 = $0.50 per unit of output. If the machine produces 1,000 units of output during the first period, the depreciation expense for that period would be: 1,000 × $0.50 = $500. Depending upon output, depreciation expense would be different for subsequent periods.

3. Sum-of-the-years'-digits method—This approach is called accelerated depreciation. A greater amount of depreciation is recorded in each year than in the following year.

Example: The depreciation for each of the five years for the above asset is computed by using a decreasing fraction as follows:

103

Year	Fraction*	Computation	Depreciation Expense
1	5/15	× $3,000 =	$1,000
2	4/15	× 3,000 =	800
3	3/15	× 3,000 =	600
4	2/15	× 3,000 =	400
5	1/15	× 3,000 =	200
15	—Sum of the digits is the denominator.		$3,000

*Numerator is the years in inverse order and denominator is the sum of the years (col. 1 above).

(a) The denominator of the ratio can be computed by using the formula:

$$SYD = n\left(\frac{n+1}{2}\right)$$

4. Declining-balance method—The acceleration rate used is a percent of the straight-line rate and residual value is **excluded** from the base to be depreciated (except that the total amount depreciated over the life of the asset cannot exceed cost less residual value). The acceleration rates are prescribed by income tax regulations. The rate may be as high as 200 percent of the straight-line rate.

Example of 200 percent acceleration rate: The straight-line depreciation rate above was 20 percent (based on a 5-year life) and the acceleration rate is 200 percent, therefore the declining rate would be 40 percent. This rate is multiplied at the end of each year by the previous book value of the asset. Depreciation stops when the book value equals the estimated residual value. The above asset would be depreciated as follows:

Year	Computations	Depreciation Expense	Book Value (End of Year)	
At acquisition:				$3,500
1	40%* × $3,500 =	$1,400	($3,500 − $1,400) =	2,100
2	40% × $2,100 =	840	($2,100 − $ 840) =	1,260
3	40% × $1,260 =	504	($1,260 − $ 504) =	756
4	$756 − $500 =	256**	($ 756 − $ 256) =	500

*200% × 20% = 40%

**Depreciation stops when book value equals the estimated residual value.

5. Depreciation for tax purposes. Most companies use the Modified Accelerated Cost Recovery System (MACRS) to calculate depreciation expense on their tax returns. MACRS is not used for financial accounting purposes. This method utilizes depreciation schedules that are published by the Internal Revenue Service.

F. Depreciation for short time periods, such as one month, is computed to be a proportionate part of the annual amount. For example, if the annual depreciation is $840, the monthly depreciation during that year would be $70 (i.e., $840 ÷ 12 months).

G. Changes in depreciation estimates—When an estimate is revised, the remaining undepreciated asset balance, less any residual value, is depreciated over the remaining life, based on the new estimate. Depreciation is based on two estimates:

1. Estimated useful life

2. Estimated residual value.

Example: After six years of useful life, the account balances related to Machine A were: cost at acquisition, $11,000, accumulated depreciation (based on a 10 year life and $1,000 residual value), $10,000 × 6/10 = $6,000; thus, the book (carrying) value was $5,000. At the start of year 7, the total estimated life was changed to 13 years and the estimated residual value was changed to $800. Straight-line depreciation is used.

Entries:
(a) At start of year 7—No journal entry needed.
(b) At end of year 7, adjusting entry:

Depreciation expense...................	600	
Accumulated depreciation		600

Computation:

Cost at acquisition	$11,000
Accumulated depreciation to date of change	6,000
Book value at date of change	5,000
Estimated residual value, new estimate	800
Remaining amount to be depreciated.................	$4,200

Annual depreciation $4,200 ÷ (13 years—6 years) = $600

H.   A **capital expenditure** is a cost that will benefit more than one accounting period. For example, the purchase of a machine having an estimated life of ten years often is referred to as a capital expenditure because it benefits more than one year. At acquisition date, its cost is debited to an asset account. In contrast, a **revenue expenditure** is an outlay that will benefit only one accounting period. For example, a minor routine repair expenditure is recorded as an expense because it tends to benefit only the current period.

I.   In using operational assets, expenditures must be made for repairs. Accounting recognizes two kinds of repairs:

1.   Ordinary repairs—routine, recurring, and usual expenditures made to keep an asset, such as a machine, in operating condition. Because of these characteristics such repairs are classified as revenue expenditures and are debited to repair expense when incurred.

2.   Extraordinary repairs—major, nonrecurring repair expenditures. When incurred, they are debited to the asset account for the item repaired and subsequently are depreciated over the remaining life of that asset. They are the kind of renovations that occur infrequently, involve relatively large expenditures, and tend to increase the economic usefulness of the asset. Such repairs are classified as capital expenditures. The replacement of an old roof on a building with a new and improved roof would be an extraordinary repair.

J.   Disposal of operational assets requires that (1) the original cost of the asset be removed from the accounts, (2) the related accumulated depreciation amount be removed, (3) the consideration received for it be recorded, and (4) a loss or gain on disposal be recognized.

Example: An operational asset that showed the following in the accounts is sold:

Machine acquisition cost (a debit)	$2,000
Accumulated depreciation (a credit)	1,200

The machine was sold for $600 cash. The journal entry to record the disposal is:

Cash.	600	
Accumulated depreciation	1,200	
Loss on sale of operational asset	200	
Machinery		2,000

K. A natural resource often is referred to as a "wasting asset." When acquired, natural resources are recorded at their cash equivalent price in conformity with the cost principle. Natural resources are subject to depletion as they are used or exploited (in accordance with the matching principle).

Example: A gravel pit was acquired at a cost of $20,000. It is estimated that 100,000 cubic yards of gravel can be taken from it and a $5,000 residual value is expected. The depletion rate would be: $15,000 ÷ 100,000 = $0.15 per cubic yard. Assuming 5,000 cubic yards are removed during the year, the depletion for that year is recorded as follows:

Depletion expense ($0.15 × 5,000)	750	
Gravel pit (or Accumulated depletion, gravel pit)		750

L. Intangible operational assets are recorded at their cash equivalent cost when acquired. They are subject to amortization of the full acquisition cost over their remaining useful life. They seldom, if ever, have a residual value.

Example: A patent is acquired at a cost of $600, five years after it was registered. Thus, it has a remaining life of 12 years. Amortization of the acquisition cost is recorded each year as follows:

Patent amortization expense	50	
Patent ($600 ÷ 12 years)		50

9—Questions for Self Evaluation

These questions follow the sequence of the discussions in the chapter. However, they do not cover all of the points discussed in the chapter. After studying the chapter, try to answer each question to the best of your ability without referring again to the chapter. After answering all of them, turn to the solutions in the back and evaluate yourself. This should provide a valuable guide for deciding how much additional study you should commit to the chapter.

1. Operational assets always are noncurrent and always are used in normal operations.

   _____ T; _____ F

2. Operational assets basically are reported in conformity with the (a) _____ and (b) _____ principles.

3. Those noncurrent assets that a business retains more or less permanently for use in the business usually are called _____ .

4. At acquisition an operational asset is recorded as an (a) _____ , and over its useful life its cost periodically is matched with revenue as (b) _____ .

5. Under the cost principle, the acquisition cost of an operational asset is its _____ _____ .

6. Company B purchased a machine (operational asset), and made the following payments on it: cash $50,000 and issued 5,000 shares of its own nopar stock to the seller (market value was $15 per share). In addition, installation and sales taxes on the machine amounted to $3,000 cash. The seller paid transportation costs of $4,100. Give the journal entry to record the acquisition.

   _____ _____ _____

   _____ _____ _____

   _____ _____ _____

   _____ _____ _____

   _____ _____ _____

7. Company P owns a machine that cost $12,000 when purchased new. The machine is two thirds depreciated at the present date and has no residual value. It currently is quoted on the used market at $6,500. What amount should be reported as its book value on the balance sheet at this date?

   (a) $_____ . What is its current market value? (b) $_____ .

8. Company X purchased two tracts of land for a single sum of $32,000. In addition, it paid $1,000 for transfer costs and fees. The land was assessed for tax purposes as follows: Tract A—$13,000; Tract B—$7,000. What amount should be recorded as the acquisition price of:

   Tract A? $_____ . Tract B? $_____ .

9. Intangible operating assets have value only because they confer certain rights to the owner, although they do have physical substance. _____ T; _____ F

10. Tangible operational assets have both physical substance and related rights. _____ T; _____ F

11. The apportionment of the purchase cost of an operational asset to the future periods in which the benefits of its use contribute to the earning of periodic revenue is required by the _____ _____ principle.

12. Match the following terms with the brief descriptions:

Description		Term
(a) _____ An intangible asset		A. Depletion
(b) _____ A natural resource		B. Depreciation
(c) _____ A machine used in the factory		C. Amortization
		D. None of the above
(d) _____ A tract of land (used as the company parking lot)		

13. A machine cost $8,000; its estimated useful life is 5 years and the residual value is 10 percent of its cost. Show how its effects should be reported on the (a) balance sheet and (b) income statement at the end of the third year. Assume straight-line depreciation.

(a) _____

_____

_____

_____

(b) _____

_____

14. The adjusting entry, at the end of each period, on an operational asset is required because of the _____ principle.

15. What three amounts must be known or estimated to compute depreciation expense?

(a) The known amount: _____ .

(b) An estimated amount: _____ .

(c) An estimated use factor: _____ .

16. Repairs that occur infrequently, involve relatively large expenditures, and tend to increase the economic usefulness of the asset are called (a) _____ repairs; all other repairs are called (b) _____ repairs.

17. During the year Company T spent $400 for usual, recurring repairs on the building and $3,500 for the major overhaul of a machine. Give the required journal entry.

18. Company A has a machine that originally cost $4,800 (no residual value). It is being depreciated, on a straight-line basis, over an estimated useful life of six years. Shortly after the end of the fourth year it was sold for $1,900. Give the journal entry to record the sale.

19. (Based on Supplement 9B) Company E owns Asset X that cost $10,000. The accumulated depreciation on it is $3,000. Asset X is traded for Asset Y and $1,500 cash boot is paid. The market value of Asset X, when traded, was $7,300. Give the journal entry to record the transaction, assuming:

CASE A—Assets X and Y were similar:

CASE B—Assets X and Y were dissimilar:

20. Company K acquired a mineral deposit at a cost of $6,000,000. It is estimated that production amounting to 10 million units can be economically withdrawn from it. During the first year 800,000 units were withdrawn.

(a) The depletion rate is _____ per unit.

(b) Depletion expense for the first year is $ _____.

(c) The adjusting entry at the end of the first year is:

_____ _____ _____

_____ _____ _____

_____ _____ _____

21. Company T purchased a patent at a cost of $16,800 three years after it was registered. The company estimated the total economic life (from date of registration) was 15 years. Give the adjusting entry at the end of the first year after purchase.

_____ _____ _____

_____ _____ _____

_____ _____ _____

22. Match each definition with the intangible asset designation.

Definition   *Designation*

(a) _____ The right to publish, use, and sell a literary, musical, or artistic work   A. Deferred charge

(b) _____ The right to use specified property for a future period of time because of the payment of cash rent in advance   B. Leasehold

(c) _____ The amount paid for the customer confidence and general reputation of a business   C. Copyright

(d) _____ A long-term prepaid expense   D. Goodwill

E. Patent

(e) _____ Buildings, alterations, and other construction made by the lessee on leased property   F. Franchise

(f) _____ An open account owed to the company by a customer   G. Leasehold improvement

(g) _____ A right, granted by another party, to use a designation (such as Superburger) or to distribute a product in a given area, for a specified period of time   H. None of the above

(h) _____ An exclusive right to use and market an invention

23. At acquisition, intangible assets are measured and recorded in accordance with the (a) _____ principle and are amortized over (b) _____ .

24. A "wasting asset" such as a mineral deposit or a timber tract is called a (a) _____ . As consumed, or used up, cost is apportioned to each period when related revenue is measured. This is known as (b) _____ .

112

25. A building cost $80,000. The estimated useful life is 30 years. At the end of the useful life it is estimated that the building will cost $1,000 to tear down and that the scrap can be sold for $2,400. Give the adjusting entry at the end of year 1 assuming straight-line depreciation.

_____   _____   _____

_____   _____   _____

_____   _____   _____

26. Complete the following tabulation for an asset that cost $1,200 and has an estimated residual life of $300.

Depreciation Method	Useful Life	Depreciation Expense—Year 1	
		Computations	Amount/Year
(a) Straight line	4 years		
(b) Productive output (production in year one, 300 units)	1,000 units		
(c) Sum-of-the-years' digits	4 years		
(d) 200 percent acceleration rate	4 years		

27. Define each of the following terms:

(a) Capital expenditure: _____

_____

_____

(b) Revenue expenditure: _____

_____

_____

28. Match each of the following accounting terms with its proper definition by inserting the letter which identifies the definition in the space next to the term.

Accounting Terms	*Definitions*
____ (1) Acquisition cost	A. Assets used in the operations of a business that have special rights but not physical substance
____ (2) Amortization	B. Systematic and rational apportionment of the cost of a tangible operational asset over its useful life
____ (3) Basket purchase	
____ (4) Book (or carrying) value	C. Expenditures that are debited to an expense account; the incurrence of an expense
____ (5) Capital expenditures	D. Expenditures that are debited to an asset account; the acquisition of an asset
____ (6) Capitalization of interest	E. Systematic and rational apportionment of the cost of a natural resource over the period of exploitation
____ (7) Copyrights	
____ (8) Declining balance	F. Estimated service life of an operational asset to the present owner
____ (9) Deferred charges	G. Exclusive right to publish, use, and sell a literary, musical, or artistic work
____ (10) Depletion	
____ (11) Depreciation	H. Estimated amount to be recovered less disposal costs, at the end of the estimated useful life of an operational asset
____ (12) Estimated residual value	
____ (13) Estimated useful life	I. Acquisition cost of the purchase of a business that is in excess of the market value of the net assets of the business purchased
____ (14) Extraordinary repairs	
____ (15) Goodwill	J. Interest expenditures included in the cost of an operational asset; during construction period
____ (16) Intangible operational assets	K. Net cash equivalent amount paid for an asset
____ (17) Leaseholds	L. Expenditures by the lessee on leased property which has use value beyond the current accounting period
____ (18) Leasehold improvements	
____ (19) Operational assets	M. Cost of an operational asset is allocated over its useful life based upon a fraction where the denominator is the total of all of the useful years and the numerator is the years of life in inverse order
____ (20) Productive output depreciation	
____ (21) Repairs and maintenance	
____ (22) Residual value	N. Cost of an operational asset is allocated over its useful life based upon the periodic output related to total estimated output
____ (23) Revenue expenditures	
____ (24) Straight-line depreciation	O. An accelerated depreciation method based upon a multiple of the straight-line rate; it disregards residual value
____ (25) Sum-of-years'-digits depreciation	
____ (26) Tangible operational assets	P. Estimated service life of an operational asset to the present owner
____ (27) Useful life of an operational asset	Q. Expenditures for normal operating upkeep of operational assets; debit expense for ordinary repairs
	R. An expense paid in advance of usage of the goods or services; long-term prepayment

S. Cost of an operational asset is allocated over its useful life in equal periodic amounts

T. Rights granted to a lessee under a lease contract

U. Acquisition of two or more assets in a single transaction for a single lump sum

V. Estimated amount to be recovered less disposal costs, at the end of the estimated useful life of an operational asset

W. Asset used in the operations of a business that has physical substance

X. Major, high cost, and long-term repairs; debited to an asset account (or accumulated depreciation)

Y. Systematic and rational apportionment of the cost of an intangible operational asset over its useful life

Z. Tangible and intangible assets owned by a business and used in its operations

AA. Acquisition cost of an operational asset less accumulated depreciation, depletion or amortization

10

Measuring and Reporting Liabilities

PURPOSE OF THIS CHAPTER

A business generates or receives resources from three sources: (a) capital contributions by owners, (b) income from operations, and (c) borrowing from creditors. Creditors provide resources by making cash loans and by selling property, goods, and services on credit. For users of financial statements, the liabilities reported on the balance sheet, and the related interest expense reported on the income statement, are important factors in evaluating the financial performance of a business. The purpose of this chapter is to discuss the measurement, recording, and reporting of liabilities and the related interest expense.

HOW TO STUDY THIS CHAPTER

This chapter discusses the measuring, recording, and reporting of short-term and long-term liabilities. Part A considers the different kinds of liabilities and Part B discusses the concepts of present and future value (i.e., the time value of money—interest). We suggest that the illustrations be studied carefully. You will find that some of the concepts discussed were introduced in earlier chapters (such as the computation of interest and the adjusting entry for accrued interest expense).

Part B of the chapter, involving present and future values, is fairly sophisticated. However, if you study it carefully, including the illustrations, you will find that it is relatively easy to comprehend. We emphasize that these concepts are important in a wide range of management decisions. We suggest that you work as many of the Exercises on this topic given at the end of the chapter as time permits.

STUDY OUTLINE OF THIS CHAPTER

Part A—Measuring, Recording, and Reporting Liabilities

A. Liabilities are probable future sacrifices of economic benefits arising from present obligations to transfer assets or provide services in the future as a result of past transactions or events.

   1. Liabilities are classified as either current liabilities or long-term liabilities.

2. For accounting purposes, all commercial liabilites are assumed to incur interest, whether specified or not.

B. Conceptually, liabilities are measured at their current cash equivalent amount, which is the **present value** of all future outlays required.

   1. Liabilities are recorded in conformity with the cost principle; that is, the amount of a liability is the cash equivalent of the resources received when the liability was incurred.

C. Current liabilities are short-term liabilities that are due within the current operating (i.e., cash) cycle of the business or within one year of the balance sheet, whichever is the longer. Thus, current liabilities reported on the current balance sheet are expected to be paid out of the current assets reported on the same balance sheet.

   1. The most common current liability is accounts payable, which results from purchases of goods (merchandise) acquired for resale.

   2. Numerous current liabilities arise as a result of end-of-the-period adjusting entries. Usual examples are: wages payable, taxes payable, and deferred revenues (see E below).

D. Working capital is the difference between current assets and current liabilities.

   1. The current ratio is current assets divided by current liabilities.

      Example:

Current assets............	$300,000
Current liabilities.........	100,000
Working capital	$200,000

      $$\text{Current ratio} = \frac{\text{Current assets}}{\text{Current liabilities}} = \frac{\$300,000}{\$100,000} = 3 \text{ to } 1.$$

      Thus, for each $1 of current liabilities, there are $3 of current assets.

E. A deferred revenue (i.e., a revenue collected in advance such as precollected rent revenue) is a current liability because there is a short-term obligation to render the rental service for which the cash already has been collected.

Example: On December 1, 19A, T Company collected three months rent in advance, 3 × $200 = $600. The annual accounting period ends December 31. The journal entry to record the precollected rent revenue is:

        December 1, 19A:
          Cash 600
              Rent revenue collected in advance   600

The adjusting entry on December 31, 19A, to record the rent which was earned is:

        December 31, 19A:
          Rent revenue collected in advance 200
              Rent revenue   200

F. Long-term liabilities encompass all debts and obligations not properly classifed as current liabilities (as defined in C above). They are reported under a separate subcaption on the balance sheet called long-term liabilities.

G. Bonds payable and long-term notes payable are typical long-term liabilities. Bonds and notes payable legally require the payment of interest (i.e., an expense) in contrast with capital stock issued (on which dividends usually are paid, which is not an expense).

1. Interest expense must be accrued (for all interest not yet paid or recorded) at the end of each accounting period by means of an adjusting entry.

2. Illustration of long-term note payable:

    (a) On September 1, 19E, Company X gave a $3,000, three-year, long-term, interest-bearing note for cash. Interest was specified at 12 percent per year and is payable each August 31. The journal entry to record the note is:

        Cash 3,000
            Long-term note payable (12%)   3,000

    (b) Adjusting entry at December 31, 19E for accrued interest (end of annual accounting period):

        Interest expense ($3,000 × 12% × 4/12) 120
            Interest payable   120

(c) Payment of annual interest on August 31, 19F (assuming no reversing entry on January 1, 19F):

Interest expense ($3,000 × 12% × 8/12)	240	
Interest payable (per entry b)	120	
Cash ($3,000 × 12%)		360

H. Noninterest-bearing notes are a misnomer because all notes include interest. In the case of a noninterest-bearing note, the interest is included in the face amount of the note.

Example: ABC Company borrowed money on January 1, 19A and agreed to repay $1,100 on December 31, 19A. The company signed a "noninterest-bearing" note.

(a) January 1, 19A—borrowed money

Cash	1,000	
Discount on note payable	100	
Note payable		1,100

(b) December 31, 19A—repaid note

Note payable	1,100	
Interest expense	100	
Discount on note payable..................		100
Cash..		1,100

I. Deferred taxes are caused by the difference between taxable income (reported on the tax return) and pretax income (reported on the income statement).

(a) Temporary differences are taxable revenues or tax deductible expenses that are reported on the tax return in one accounting period and the income statement in a different period. Each temporary difference creates either a deferred tax liability or a deferred tax asset.

(b) Income tax expense is computed as follows:

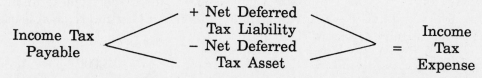

(c) Deferred tax liabilities and assets (based on temporary differences) originate in one accounting period and reverse (have the opposite effect) in some subsequent period.

120

J. A **contingent liability** is not a legal or effective liability. It is a **potential future liability**. It arises because of an event that already has happened, which may cause a future liability depending on a future event that has not yet happened. For example, if a company is sued for damages, a contingent liability arises. There will be no legal liability unless the lawsuit is lost and damages must be paid. At a future time, if the lawsuit is lost, a legal liability comes into existence. If the lawsuit is won, the contingent liability no longer exists. During the period between the filing and final determination of the lawsuit, a contingent liability exists. The contingent liability usually is not recorded in the accounting system. During the period of its existence, it is reported on the financial statements by means of a note to the financial statements. When a contingent liability becomes a reasonably probable loss, a liability is recorded (e.g., debit loss and credit liability).

K. Voucher system—a procedure that requires a written authorization (called a voucher) for any transaction that creates a legal obligation to make an expenditure of cash .

1. The voucher system replaces the cash disbursements journal (supplement 8B).
2. The objective of the voucher system is to obtain greater internal control.

Part B—Present Value and Future Value Concepts

L. The concepts of present and future value relate to the time value of money or interest (which is the cost of using money). When money is loaned or borrowed, there is an interest charge determined by (1) the amount of the principal, (2) the interest rate, and (3) the length of time of the loan.

There are four different present and future value concepts involving interest. In order to save computational time, present and future value tables, based on $1, have been developed for each of the four concepts as follows:

Table Name	Symbol	Table Number in Textbook
1. Future value of $1	f	10-1
2. Present value of $1.........................	p	10-2
3. Future value of annuity of $1	F	10-3
4. Present value of annuity of $1	P	10-4

M. Explanation of the four present and future value concepts:

1. Future value of $1—the future dollar amount that $1 will increase to at i interest rate for n periods of time. The future amount will be the principal (i.e., $1) plus compound interest.

   Application:
   Company T decided to deposit $20,000 in a special savings fund that will earn 10 percent interest, which will be added to the fund.

   (a) How much will be in the fund at the end of Year 3?

   Answer (refer to Table 10-1 in the textbook):

   $$\$20,000 \times f_{n=3 \atop i=10\%} (1.3310) = \underline{\$26,620}.$$

   (b) Construct a table to show the growth of this fund.

   Answer:

Year	Amount at Start of Year	+ Interest During the Year =	Fund Balance at End of Year
1	$20,000	$20,000 × 10% = $2,000	$22,000
2	22,000	22,000 × 10% = 2,200	24,200
3	24,200	24,200 × 10% = 2,420	26,620

   (c) Give the required journal entries.

   Answer:

   (1) Start of year 1—Establish fund:

   Special fund 20,000
   Cash 20,000

122

(2) End of year—Record interest:

	Year 1		Year 2		Year 3
Special fund	2,000		2,200		2,420
Interest revenue		2,000		2,200	2,420

2. Present value of $1—the dollar value now of $1 to be received at a date n periods in the future, discounted back to the present date at i interest rate.

Application:
Company V purchased a used machine on January 1, 19A. Because Company V was short of cash the seller agreed to full payment of the $10,000 price on December 31, 19B, with no addition for interest (even though the going rate of interest was 10 percent per year).

(a) What was the cost of the machine to Company V in conformity with the cost principle?

Answer (refer to Table 10-2 in the textbook):

$$\$10,000 \times p_{n=2}\ (0.8264) = \underline{\$8,264}.$$
$$i=10\%$$

(b) How much interest expense did Company V pay in Year 1, $ _____ , Year 2, $ _____ , Total $ _____ ?

Answer (rounded to nearest dollar):

Year 1, $8,264 × 10% = $826; Year 2, ($8,264 + $826) × 10% = $910.

Total interest: $10,000 − $8,264 = $1,736 (proof: $826 + $910 = $1,736).

3. Future value of annuity of $1—the future dollar amount that will be on hand at the end of n periods if $1 is deposited *each* of the n periods at i interest rate. The final amount given in the annuity table is at the date of the last deposit.

Application:
Company W deposited $1,000 in a special fund on December 31, 19A through 19C (i.e., three periods and three deposits). The fund balance will earn 10 percent interest per year which is added to the fund (i.e., compound interest).

(a) What amount will be in the fund on December 31, 19C, end of year 3?

Answer (refer to Table 10-3 in the textbook):

$$\$1,000 \times F_{n=3}\ (3.3100) = \underline{\$3,310}.$$
$$i=10\%$$

(b) How much interest will the fund earn over the three years?

Answer:

$3,310 - ($1,000 \times 3) = \underline{\$310}$.

(c) Prepare a table to show the growth of this fund.

Answer:

End of Year	Annual Deposit	Interest on Fund Balance	Fund Balance at Year End
1	$1,000	None	$1,000
2	1,000	$1,000 \times 10\% = $100	$1,000 + $100 = 2,100
3	1,000	$2,100 \times 10\% = 210	$2,100 + $1,000 + $210 = 3,310

4. Present value of annuity of $1—the dollar amount now of a series of future equal amounts to be received each period for *n* number of periods in the future, discounted at *i* rate of interest. It is the inverse of future value (3) above, therefore, it involves compound discounting (from the future to the present).

Application:
On January 1, 19A, Company X purchased an asset which has a useful life of three years and no residual value. This asset will pay back $10,000 cash at the end of each of the three years (19A, B, and C). The "going" rate of interest is 10 percent per year.

(a) How much should Company X be willing to pay for this asset assuming that a 10 percent rate of return is expected (disregard income tax implications)?

Answer (refer to Table 10-4 in the textbook):

$$\$10,000 \times P_{n=3 \atop i=10\%} \ (2.4869) = \underline{\$24,869}.$$

(b) How much total interest would this investment earn?

Answer:

$(\$10,000 \times 3) - \$24,869 = \underline{\$5,131}$.

Another application: J. Doe purchased a new car, cost $15,000, of which $5,000 cash was paid. The $10,000 balance was financed at 20 percent over 5 years (payments at the end of each year).

(a) What would be the amount of each annual payment?

Answer:

$$\$10,000 \div P_{n=5 \atop i=20\%} \ (2.9906) = \underline{\$3,344} \ \text{(rounded)}.$$

(b) How much total interest will be paid?

Answer:

$$(\$3,344 \times 5) - \$10,000 = \underline{\$6,720}.$$

N. Lease liabilities—there are two different types of leases:

(1) Operating lease—short-term lease wherein the lessor (i.e., owner) agrees to let the lessee (i.e., renter) use property (such as an office) for a stipulated monthly (or other period) rental payment. Importantly, the lessor continues to be responsible for paying all ownership costs (e.g., taxes, insurance, and major repairs). The only lease entries by the lessor and lessee are for the rentals as follows:

March 1, 19A—payment of March rental of $500:

	Lessor	Lessee
Cash	500	500
Rent expense		500
Rent revenue	500	

(2) Capital lease—long-term noncancelable lease wherein the lessor (owner) transfers to the lessee (renter) most of the risks and rewards of ownership (e.g., the lessee controls and uses the property) and also pays the ownership costs; (e.g., taxes, insurance and all repairs). Periodic rental payments are made. These conditions cause a capital lease to be, in effect, an installment sale of the leased property by the lessor to the lessee. Thus, journal entries must be made by both parties as follows:

(a) At lease date:
Lessor—records a sale of the leased property
Lessee—records a purchase of the leased property

(b) At each rental payment date:
Lessor—records collection on a receivable (including interest)
Lessee—records payment on a liability (including interest)

10—Questions for Self Evaluation

These questions follow the sequence of the discussions in the chapter. However, they do not cover all of the points discussed in the chapter. After studying the chapter, try to answer each question to the best of your ability without referring again to the chapter. After answering all of them, turn to the solutions in the back and evaluate yourself. This should provide a valuable guide for deciding how much additional study you should commit to the chapter.

1. Liabilities are defined as probable future sacrifices of _____

    arising from present obligations to transfer _____

    or provide services in the future as a result of _____

    _____ .

2. Liabilities are classified on the balance sheet as either (a) _____ or

    (b) _____ .

3. Fundamentally, liabilities are measured in conformity with the _____ principle.

4. The amount of a liability and the maturity date are always known. _____ T; _____ F

5. Current liabilities are short-term obligations that will be paid within _____

    _____ or within

    _____

    whichever is _____ .

6. An accrued liability arises because of an _____ that already has been incurred

    but is not yet _____ .

7. All commercial liabilities incur interest, whether specified or not. _____ T; _____ F

8. Company Z reported total current assets of $60,000 and total current liabilities of $20,000. Therefore,

    (a) working capital was $ _____ , and (b) the working capital ratio was _____ .

9. Current liabilities include all obligations due within one year from the balance sheet date. _____ T;

    _____ F

10. At the end of the annual accounting period, December 31, 19A, wages earned but not paid or recorded amounted to $780. Disregard payroll taxes.

(a) Give the adjusting entry (including the appropriate date).

_____ _____ _____
_____ _____ _____
_____ _____ _____

(b) On January 10, 19B, wages paid for the payroll period, December 28, 19A, to January 10, 19B, amounted to $11,900 that included the $780 unpaid in December 19A. Give the journal entry (with appropriate date).

_____ _____ _____
_____ _____ _____
_____ _____ _____
_____ _____ _____

11. On June 30, 19A, Company N paid the monthly payroll. The amounts were: cash, $15,900; wages paid, $20,000; income tax withheld, $2,500; union dues withheld, $400; and FICA taxes, $1,200. Give the journal entry.

_____ _____ _____
_____ _____ _____
_____ _____ _____
_____ _____ _____
_____ _____ _____
_____ _____ _____

12. A revenue collected in advance of the period in which it will be earned also is called _____
_____.

13. On December 15, 19A, Company X collected $3,500 rent revenue in advance for the following 30 days. The accounting period ends on December 31. The collection was recorded as a debit to cash and a credit to rent revenue. Give the adjusting entry on December 31, 19A.

_____ _____ _____
_____ _____ _____
_____ _____ _____

14. A secured debt is characterized by the fact that the borrower has _____ as security for the liability.

15. On February 1, 19A, Company T borrowed $1,000 on a six-month, 10 percent, interest-bearing note for that amount. Interest is payable at maturity.

(a) Give the journal entry at the date of the note.

_____ _____ _____

_____ _____ _____

_____ _____ _____

(b) Give the journal entry at the maturity date.

_____ _____ _____

_____ _____ _____

_____ _____ _____

_____ _____ _____

16. Company B executed a $3,000, 12 percent, interest-bearing, one-year note payable on August 1, 19A. The annual accounting period ends December 31. Give the entries on the following dates:

(a) August 1, 19A—date of the note.

_____ _____ _____

_____ _____ _____

_____ _____ _____

(b) December 31, 19A—adjusting entry for accrued interest.

_____ _____ _____

_____ _____ _____

_____ _____ _____

(c) July 31, 19B—payment of the note plus interest. Assume that no reversing entry was made on January 1, 19B.

_____ _____ _____

_____ _____ _____

_____ _____ _____

_____ _____ _____

17. Company R, reported $2,000 investment revenue on the 19A income tax return but reported it on the 19B income statement (per GAAP). Therefore, deferred income tax should be recorded for 19A as (assume a 30 percent income tax rate) a:

    A. Debit, $600.
    B. Credit, $600.
    C. Debit, $2,000.
    D. Credit, $2,000.
    E. None of the above, it should be _____.

18. A revenue or expense that is never entered on a tax return (i.e., nontaxable items) does not cause deferred income taxes to be recorded. _____ T; _____ F

19. The deferred income tax account balance never will be a debit. _____ T; _____ F

20. Deferred income taxes may be reported as either an asset or a liability depending upon the circumstances. _____ T; _____ F

21. Temporary differences will always reverse. _____ T; _____ F

22. Company X reported pretax income for 19A and 19B as follows: 19A—$20,000; 19B—$35,000. Assume an income tax rate of 30 percent. A $5,000 expense was deducted on the income statement in 19A but it was deducted on the income tax return for 19B. Give the journal entries to record income tax expense, deferred tax, and income tax payable for each year.

19A:

_____ _____ _____

_____ _____ _____

_____ _____ _____

_____ _____ _____

19B:

_____ _____ _____

_____ _____ _____

_____ _____ _____

_____ _____ _____

23. A contingent liability is a potential future liability that has arisen as a result of an event that has

_____; however, its conversion to an effective liability is dependent upon

the _____

_____.

24. A contingent liability is not recorded in the accounts but nevertheless is reported on the financial statements. _____ T; _____ F

25. The time value of money is another name for _____. What is the time value of money for $2,000 for one year assuming an 8 percent rate of interest?

_____

26. Match each of the following concepts with its definition by entering the appropriate code letter to the left.

Definition	Concept
(a) _____ The present amount of n periodic payments of $1 to be received (or paid) in each of the future periods, discounted at i interest rate.	A. Future value of $1
	B. Present value of $1
(b) _____ The future amount of $1 for n periods at i interest rate.	C. Future value of annuity of $1
(c) _____ The present amount of $1 due n periods hence, discounted at i interest rate.	D. Present value of annuity of $1
(d) _____ The future amount of n periodic contributions of $1 each plus compound interest at i interest rate.	

27. To solve the following problem use tables from the textbook (Tables 10-1 through 10-4):

(a) If at the start of Year 1, Company A deposited $1,500 in a fund at 8 percent interest, what would be the balance in the fund at the end of the sixth year assuming the interest earned is added to the fund? Show computations.

_____ = $ _____

(b) Company B deposited $1,500 each year in a fund at 8 percent interest. Assuming interest earned is added to fund, what would be the fund balance immediately after the sixth deposit? Show computations.

_____ = $ _____

(c) There is an arrangement whereby Company C will have to pay $50,000 five years from now. Assuming a going rate of interest of 15 percent, what could the company settle the debt for now? Show computations.

_____ = $ _____

(d) Assume you own a piece of property and can rent it for $2,000 per year for four years. The annual rent is collectible at the end of each year. Assuming an 8 percent annual interest rate, what single amount would you accept at the start of Year 1 (now) instead of waiting for the four payments? Show computations.

_____ = $ _____

28. At the beginning of Year 1, Company K set aside $100,000 in a special building fund. The fund will be used at the end of 10 years to pay for the building. Assume 7 percent interest per year.

(a) What amount will be in the fund at the end of the 10th year? $_____ .

(b) Give the journal entry to record the deposit of the cash in the fund at the beginning of Year 1.

_____ _____ _____

_____ _____ _____

_____ _____ _____

131

(c) Give the journal entry for interest revenue at the end of Year 1.

_____   _____   _____

_____   _____   _____

_____   _____   _____

(d) Give the journal entry for interest revenue at the end of Year 2.

_____   _____   _____

_____   _____   _____

_____   _____   _____

(e) What will be the balance in the fund at the start of Year 3?

_____

_____

29. The future value of an annuity of $1 for $n = 10$; $i = 11\%$, will be more than $10. _____ T; _____ F

30. Assume you purchased a swordfish sail boat which cost $35,000. You paid $5,000 cash and signed a 4-year, 10 percent interest-bearing note. Assuming equal annual payments at each year end (i.e., 4 payments), each annual payment would be (a) $ _____ , and your total interest cost would be (b) $ _____ .

31. Match each of the following accounting terms with its proper definition by inserting the letter which identifies the definition in the space next to the term.

Accounting Terms

_____ (1) Accrued expenses

_____ (2) Annuity

_____ (3) Capital lease

_____ (4) Contingent liability

_____ (5) Current liabilities

_____ (6) Current ratio

_____ (7) Deferred income tax

_____ (8) Deferred revenues

_____ (9) Future value

_____ (10) Interest-bearing note

_____ (11) Liabilities

_____ (12) Long-term liabilities

_____ (13) Noninterest-bearing note

_____ (14) Operating lease

_____ (15) Present value

_____ (16) Temporary difference

_____ (17) Time value of money

_____ (18) Working capital

Definitions

A. The ratio of current assets divided by current liabilities.

B. The value now of an amount to be received in the future

C. Expenses that have been incurred but have not yet been paid or recorded at the end of the accounting period; a liability

D. Revenues which have been collected but not earned; a liability

E. Interest which is associated with the use of borrowed money over time

F. A note that explicitly specifies a stated rate of interest

G. Probable future sacrifices of economic benefits that arise from past transactions

H. A series of periodic payment which are equal in amount

I. Differences between income tax expense and income tax payable, caused by temporary differences

J. A rental agreement between a lessor and lessee that is not viewed in accounting as a purchase/sale

K. A lease which is viewed as a purchase/sale, for accounting purposes

L. A note that does not explicitly state a rate of interest but has implicit interest; interest is included in the face amount of the note

M. The dollar difference between total current assets and total current liabilities

N. Potential liability that has arisen as the result of a past event; not an effective liability

O. All obligations not properly classified as current liabilities

P. The sum to which an amount will increase as the result of compound interest

Q. Short-term obligations that will be paid within the current operating cycle or one year, whichever is longer

R. An income tax difference that causes deferred taxes; will reverse or turn around in the future

Measuring and Reporting Bonds Payable

PURPOSE OF THIS CHAPTER

Chapter 10 discussed current liabilities and the concepts of future and present value. This chapter discusses long-term liabilities, with emphasis on bonds payable. Long-term liabilities are an important source of funds that are primarily used to purchase noncurrent assets. Bonds are long-term debt instruments. When bonds are issued (i.e., sold), they represent an investment for the buyer and a liability for the issuer. Accounting for bonds involves some complexities. The purpose of this chapter is to discuss measuring, recording, and reporting the financial effects of bonds payable on the entity.

HOW TO STUDY THIS CHAPTER

This chapter requires careful study including the illustrations. Measuring, recording, and reporting bonds payable is complicated because usually there is bond premium or discount. Accounting for interest, including the adjusting entry for accrued interest at the end of each accounting period, was presented in earlier chapters. Therefore, you should focus your attention on the measuring, recording, and reporting of bond premium and discount. Keeping track of the various bond and interest dates sometimes is troublesome. A time-scale graph, similar to that shown in Part B of the chapter, is recommended. Many students find it almost essential to sketch such a graph for each problem that they attempt to solve (particularly on examinations). The Demonstration Case is almost a "must" for this chapter.

STUDY OUTLINE OF THIS CHAPTER

Part A—Fundamentals of Measuring, Recording, and Reporting Bonds Payable

A.   Bonds payable are long-term liabilities. They usually are for terms of 10 to 30 or more years. They specify an annual rate of interest which usually is paid on a semiannual basis (i.e., one half of the annual rate). Bonds often are used to obtain funds for long-term purposes such as the acquisition of plants, buildings, and major items of machinery.

1. Important terms related to bonds are:

   (a) Principal or maturity amount—the amount payable at maturity excluding any interest (also called the par value or face amount).
   (b) Stated interest rate—the rate of interest, payable in cash at each interest date, specified in the bond contract.
   (c) Market interest rate—the interest rate that investors demand in order to buy bonds. Also called yield or effective rate of interest.
   (d) Maturity date—the date on which the principal amount must be paid.
   (e) Bond premium—any excess of the par value, or principal of bond over the sales price.
   (f) Bond discount—any excess of the par value, or principal of the bond, over the sales price.
   (g) Bond indenture—the bond contract that states the legal provisions of the bond.

2. Special characteristics and classifications of bonds—review Exhibit 11 – 1 in the text.

B. Accounting for bonds payable involves three distinct phases: (1) the issuance of the bonds, (2) accounting for the bonds during their life, and (3) the retirement of the bonds.

   1. Accounting at issuance date—The issue price of a bond includes the net cash received, plus the current market value of any noncash resources received. Net cash received is the sales price less all costs of issuing the bonds. This is the current cash equivalent amount. It is compared with the par value to determine whether the bond was sold at par, at a premium, or at a discount. At sales date, bonds payable are measured and recorded as follows, assuming $60,000 par value bonds are sold and issued (application of the cost principle):

	If the Bonds Are Issued at—		
	Par	A Discount	A Premium
At date of sale:			
Cash	60,000	58,800	61,200
Discount on bonds payable		1,200	
Premium on bonds payable			1,200
Bonds payable (11%, 10-year)....	60,000	60,000	60,000

(a) A bond is issued at a discount when the stated rate of interest is less than the market rate.
(b) A bond is issued at a premium when the stated rate of interest is more than the market rate.

2. Accounting during the life of the bonds—The interest payments must be recorded on each interest payment date, and any bond premium or discount must be amortized as an adjustment to interest expense. At the end of each period, an adjusting entry must be made for any unpaid interest and any related discount or premium amortization.

Example: Assuming annual interest on the above bonds and straight-line amortization of premium or discount, the annual interest payment would be recorded as follows (application of the matching principle):

	If the Bonds Were Issued at—		
	Par	A Discount	A Premium
On interest date:			
Interest expense	6,600	6,720	6,480
Premium on bonds payable*			120
Discount on bonds payable*		120	
Cash ($60,000 × 11%)	6,600	6,600	6,600

*$1,200 × 12/120 = $120 amortization per year for 10 years.

3. Accounting at retirement date—The bonds are paid off and the principal amount is removed from the Bonds payable account. (Note: At this date the Bond premium or Bond discount accounts will have been amortized down to a zero balance.)

   Example: Retirement of the above bonds payable (at maturity date):

Bonds payable....................................	60,000	
Cash		60,000

C. Reporting bonds payable on the balance sheet—Bonds payable are reported on the balance sheet net of any unamortized bond discount or bond premium.

   Example: The above bonds would be reported on the financial statements at the end of the first year similar to the following:

   Balance sheet:

	If the Bonds Were Issued at—		
	Par	*A Discount*	*A Premium*
Long-term liabilities:			
Bonds payable (11%, 10-year)......	$60,000	$60,000	$60,000
Less: Unamortized discount		1,080	
Add: Unamortized premium			1,080
Net liability	$60,000	$58,920	$61,080
Income statement:			
Interest expense	$ 6,600	$ 6,720	$ 6,480

D. Bonds offer several advantages to the issuer when compared to the issuance of common stock.

   1. Issuance of bonds does not dilute ownership and control of the company.

   2. Cash payments to bondholders are limited to the specified interest payments and the principal.

138

3. The net cost of borrowed funds is reduced because interest payments are a tax deductible expense.

E. There are some disadvantages associated with issuing bonds.

    1. Interest payments legally must be paid each period even if the company incurs a loss.
    2. The principal amount must be repaid on the maturity date.

Part B—Some Special Problems in Accounting for Bonds Payable

F. Accounting for bonds sold between interest dates—When bonds are sold between two interest dates, the buyer must pay to the seller the interest that has accrued since the last interest date.

    1. The amount of accrued interest must be included in the journal entry to record the sale of the bond.
    2. Any premium or discount must be amortized over the remaining period that the bonds are outstanding.

G. Accrual of bond interest—At the end of each accounting period, any accrued bond interest (incurred but not yet paid or recorded) since the last interest date must be accrued and a related amount of bond discount or premium amortized.

Example: Assume the above bond interest is payable each November 1 and that the accounting period ends on December 31. Therefore, the following adjusting entry for two months interest and two months amortization must be made each December 31:

	If the Bonds Were Issued at—		
	Par	A Discount	A Premium
Adjusting entry:			
Interest expense	1,100	1,120	1,080
Premium on bonds payable*			20
Discount on bonds payable*		20	
Interest payable ($60,000 × 11% × 2/12)	1,100	1,100	1,100

*1,200 × 2/120 = $20 amortization for two months.

H. Bond sinking funds—A special cash fund that is used to pay off the bondholders when the bonds mature. A bond sinking fund is similar to a savings account such as was illustrated in Chapter 10, Part B.

I. Effective-interest amortization—The conceptually sound method for amortizing a bond discount or bond premium.

1. The effective-interest amortization approach is preferred over the straight-line approach because it measures the effective, or true, interest expense each period. The straight-line approach is acceptable only if its use results in amounts that are not materially different from the effective-interest amounts.

2. Effective-interest amortization is based on a **debt payment schedule** as illustrated in Exhibit 11 – 5 in the textbook.

3. Interest expense is calculated by multiplying the current unpaid balance of the liability by the market rate of interest. The amortization of the bond discount or premium is the difference between the interest expense and the amount of cash interest paid (or accrued).

11—Questions for Self Evaluation

These questions follow the sequence of the discussions in the chapter. However, they do not cover all of the points discussed in the chapter. After studying the chapter, try to answer each question to the best of your ability without referring again to the chapter. After answering all of them, turn to the solutions in the back and evaluate yourself. This should provide a valuable guide for deciding how much additional study you should commit to the chapter.

1. When a corporation issues bonds, it usually engages an (a) _____ to sell them and designates a third party, called the (b) _____ , to represent the bondholders.

2. Secured bonds include a pledge of specific assets of the bond issuer as a guarantee of repayment.
    _____ T; _____ F

3. Bonds that have more than one maturity date are called _____ bonds.

4. Bonds that may be called in for early retirement at the option of the issuer are called (a) _____ bonds; those where this option is with the investor (i.e., bondholder) are called (b) _____ bonds.

5. Bonds that may be converted to other securities of the issuer at the option of the investor are called _____ bonds.

6. If a company is paying 8 percent interest on bonds payable and earns a return of 15 percent on its total assets, there is a distinct advantage to the stockholders called _____ .

7. Bonds are recorded at the issue date at their (a) _____ amount in accordance with the (b) _____ principle.

8. A bond sold at 100 is said to sell at (a) _____ ; if sold at 104, at a (b) _____ ; and if sold at 98, at a (c) _____ .

9. If a company is in the 30 percent income tax bracket and has outstanding $10,000, 8.5 percent 10-year bonds payable, the net after-tax interest rate will be _____%.

10. Below are listed some features of common stock versus bonds. Indicate by a check mark on each line whether the feature relates primarily to common stock or bonds.

Features of Stocks versus Bonds		Stocks	Bonds
(a)	The investor is in the role of an owner, not a creditor, of the issuer.		
(b)	The investor shares in the growth and prosperity of the issuer (aside from interest or dividends).		
(c)	There is a legally enforceable return paid by the issuer.		
(d)	The payments to the investor for the use of resources provided are deductible by the issuer for income tax purposes.		
(e)	The investor is guaranteed (in the absence of bankruptcy) repayment of the investment by the issuer.		
(f)	The investor shares in the growth of earnings of the issuer.		
(g)	The investor has no claim for return on the resources provided in the absence of accumulated earnings.		
(h)	Periodic payments for the time value of money are recorded by the issuer as expense.		
(i)	Distributions to the investor must be approved each time by the board of directors of the issuer.		

11. Assume a $1,000, 10-year, 12 percent bond payable dated January 1, 19A, is issued on that date for cash. Complete the following entry:

January 1, 19A	Sold at 100		Sold at 97		Sold at 102	
Cash						
Discount on bonds						
Premium on bonds						
Bonds payable						

12. When the market and stated rates on a bond are the same the bond will sell at _____ .

13. A bond will sell at a premium when the market rate is _____ than the stated rate.

14. A bond will sell at a discount when the market rate is higher than the stated rate. _____ T; _____ F

15. Bond interest expense is recorded and reported in conformity with the _____ principle.

16. Bond premium has the effect of increasing the real or effective interest rate on a bond. _____ T; _____ F

17. The periodic amortization of bond discount by the issuer is deducted from the amount of cash paid to determine the amount of interest expense for the period _____ T; _____ F

142

18. On January 1, 19A, Corporation H sold a $10,000, 9 percent (payable annually each December 31) bond, which is due in 5 years (i.e., on December 31, 19E). Give the adjusting entry required on December 31, 19A, for each of the three assumptions (straight-line amortization):

Accounts	Sold at 100		Sold at 104		Sold at 97	
Interest expense						
Bond premium						
Bond discount						
Cash						

19. Dawn Corporation issued a $1,000, 10-year bond payable that was dated January 1, 19B. The annual interest at a rate of 6 percent was payable on a semiannual basis each June 30 and December 31.

(a) Give the journal entry to record the issuance at par.

_____ _____ _____
_____ _____ _____
_____ _____ _____
_____ _____ _____

(b) Give the journal entries for the interest payments during 19B (issued at par).

June 30:

_____ _____ _____
_____ _____ _____
_____ _____ _____
_____ _____ _____

December 31:

_____ _____ _____
_____ _____ _____
_____ _____ _____
_____ _____ _____

(c) Give the journal entry to record the issuance at 94 (instead of par).

_____ _____ _____
_____ _____ _____
_____ _____ _____
_____ _____ _____

(d) Give the journal entries for the interest payments during 19B (issued at 94). Use straight-line amortization.

June 30:

_____   _____   _____

_____   _____   _____

_____   _____   _____

_____   _____   _____

December 31:

_____   _____   _____

_____   _____   _____

_____   _____   _____

_____   _____   _____

(e) Give the journal entry to record the issuance at 106.

_____   _____   _____

_____   _____   _____

_____   _____   _____

_____   _____   _____

(f) Give the journal entries for the interest payments during 19B (issued at 106). Use straight-line amortization.

June 30:

_____   _____   _____

_____   _____   _____

_____   _____   _____

_____   _____   _____

December 31:

_____   _____   _____

_____   _____   _____

_____   _____   _____

_____   _____   _____

20. Assume a $1,000, 10-year, 12 percent bond payable is issued at 95. The interest is payable annually. The nominal or stated rate of interest is (a) _____ percent, and the approximate effective or real rate of interest is (b) _____ percent. Assume straight-line amortization.

21. Block Corporation has 10 percent bonds payable outstanding with a maturity amount of $40,000. Show how these bonds should be reported on the balance sheet under each of the following two assumptions:

(a) Unamortized premium is $2,800.

_____ _____ _____
_____ _____ _____
_____ _____ _____
_____ _____ _____

(b) Unamortized discount is $2,800.

_____ _____ _____
_____ _____ _____
_____ _____ _____
_____ _____ _____

22. Straight-line amortization of bond premium or discount causes bond interest expense for each full year to be the same dollar amount. _____ T; _____ F

23. Bonds issued between interest payment dates require consideration of accrued bond interest because the investor must pay (in addition to the purchase price) accrued interest since the last interest date. _____ T; _____ F

24. Corporation T decided to issue bonds payable of $100,000. The bonds were dated January 1, 19A, and will pay 12 percent interest, payable 6 percent each June 30 and December 31. The bonds were sold on March 1, 19A, at par plus accrued interest. Give the following journal entries.

(a) March 1, 19A—Sale and issuance of the bonds:

_____ _____ _____
_____ _____ _____
_____ _____ _____
_____ _____ _____

(b) June 30, 19A—Payment of first interest:

_____ _____ _____
_____ _____ _____
_____ _____ _____
_____ _____ _____

25. Refer to question 24 above and respond to the following:

(a) How much total cash will Corporation T pay for interest during 19A? $_____

(b) For how many months were the bonds outstanding during 19A? _____ months

(c) How much bond interest expense will be reported by Corporation T on the 19A income statement? $_____

145

(d) Explain any difference between your answers to (a) and (c).

_____

_____

_____

26. When a bond is sold between interest dates, the accrued interest for the period since the last interest date must be included in the cash paid by the buyer because _____

_____

_____

_____

_____

27. On October 1, 19A, Corporation X sold and issued a $10,000, 9 percent, 5-year bond at 98. The interest is payable each March 31 and September 30. Give the following journal entries:

(a) October 1, 19A—Sale and issuance of the bond:

_____ _____ _____

_____ _____ _____

_____ _____ _____

_____ _____ _____

(b) December 31, 19A—End of annual accounting period:

_____ _____ _____

_____ _____ _____

_____ _____ _____

_____ _____ _____

28. Corporation K issued a $3,000, 8 percent, 5-year bond at 103 plus any accrued interest. The bond was dated March 1, 19A, and was issued on May 1, 19A. Interest is paid each February 28.

How much cash would the issuer receive on May 1, 19A?

A. $3,000
B. $3,240
C. $3,090

D. $3,040
E. $3,130
F. None of the above; it was $_____

29. Refer to question 28 above. How much interest expense should Corporation K report on its 19A income statement (end of accounting year, December 31)?

A. $240
B. $148
C. $173

D. $142
E. $168
F. None of the above; it is $_____

30. When a company sets aside cash in advance to pay a bond issue at maturity date, it is known as a

_____ .

146

31. A bond sinking fund of $300,000 is to be accumulated by making eight equal annual deposits. The fund will earn 7 percent compound interest which will be added to the fund annually.

(a) Select the appropriate amount from Table 10-3 and compute the amount of the annual deposit.

_____

(b) Give the journal entry to record the first deposit to the fund.

_____ _____ _____

_____ _____ _____

_____ _____ _____

(c) Give the journal entry to record the interest earned on the fund at the end of the first year.

_____ _____ _____

_____ _____ _____

_____ _____ _____

32. Company T has a bond sinking fund with a balance of $82,000 on December 31, 19B. This asset amount should be reported on the balance sheet under the caption:

_____ .

33. Boston Company issued 10 percent bonds (payable annually) with a par value of $10,000 on January 1, 19A. The bonds mature on December 31, 19B. The market rate of interest was 12 percent when the bonds were sold. Complete the following bond payment schedule (effective-interest amortization):

Date	Cash Interest Paid	Interest Expense	Effective-Interest Amortization	Net Liability
1/1/19A				$9,662
12/31/19A				
12/31/19B				

34. Match each of the following accounting terms with its proper definition by inserting the letter which identifies the definition in the space next to the term.

Accounting Terms

_____ (1) Bond certificate

_____ (2) Bond discount

_____ (3) Bond premium

_____ (4) Bond principal

_____ (5) Bond sinking fund

_____ (6) Callable bond

_____ (7) Convertible bond

_____ (8) Coupon rate of interest

_____ (9) Debenture

_____ (10) Effective-interest amortization

_____ (11) Face amount

_____ (12) Indenture

_____ (13) Net interest cost

_____ (14) Par value

_____ (15) Redeemable bond

_____ (16) Stated rate

_____ (17) Straight-line amortization

_____ (18) Trustee

Definitions

A. An unsecured bond

B. A cash fund designated for repayment of a bond upon maturity

C. Another name for bond principal

D. A bond that is sold for less than par is sold at a discount

E. The rate of cash interest per period specified in the bond contract

F. An independent party appointed to represent the bondholders

G. Interest cost, less the tax savings associated with interest expense

H. The physical bond document

I. Bond that may be called for early retirement at the option of the issuer

J. Simplified method to amortize a bond discount or premium

K. A bond that is sold for more than par is sold at a premium

L. A bond that may be converted to other securities of the issuer (usually common stock)

M. Theoretically preferred method to amortize a bond discount or premium

N. The amount payable at the maturity of the bond; face amount

O. Bond that may be turned in for early retirement at the option of the bondholder

P. Another name for the stated rate of interest

Q. Bond contract which specifies the legal provisions of the bond

12

Measuring and Reporting Owners' Equity

PURPOSE OF THIS CHAPTER

A business receives funds from a variety of sources. In the two previous chapters, we discussed accounting for funds provided by creditors (i.e., liabilities). In this chapter, we will examine measuring and reporting funds provided by the owners of a business. Accounting for owners' equity is affected by the types of business organization. Owners' equity appears somewhat differently on the balance sheets of sole proprietorships, partnerships, and corporations. However, given the same set of transactions, the total amount of owners' equity on a given date will be the same (except for income tax effects) for every type of business organization. The focus of this chapter will be primarily on the corporate form because it is the most prominent type of business entity.

HOW TO STUDY THIS CHAPTER

This chapter explains the measuring, recording, and reporting of owners' equity for a corporation. The full disclosure and cost principles provide guidance. The discussions in this chapter are fundamental. You should read the chapter carefully and study the illustrations. The Demonstration Case should be studied carefully because it illustrates the accounting for stockholders' equity in a corporation.

STUDY OUTLINE OF THIS CHAPTER

Part A—Stockholders' Equity

A.   Owners' equity is total assets less the total liabilities of a business. It is a residual amount that represents the **book value** of the claims of the owners. Owners' equity represents funds provided by the owners.

1.   Accounting for assets and liabilities is the same whether the business is organized as a sole proprietorship, partnership, or corporation. Owners' equity is accounted for somewhat differently for each type of organization.

2.   In reporting on the financial statements, the **sources** of owners' equity are emphasized in accordance with the requirements of the full disclosure principle (see Exhibit 4-5 in the textbook).

B. The two basic sources of stockholders' equity in a corporation are:

1. Contributed capital—amounts invested in the corporation by the stockholders. Often referred to as paid-in capital.
2. Retained earnings—the cumulative amount of net income earned since organization of the corporation, less cumulative losses and dividends paid to the stockholders.

C. Terms about stockholders' equity that you should know:

1. Authorized number of shares—total number that can be issued as specified by the corporation charter.
2. Issued shares—number of shares issued to date (includes outstanding shares plus treasury shares).
3. Outstanding shares—shares currently owned by stockholders.
4. Treasury shares—shares once issued and repurchased by the issuing corporation, and still held.
5. Subscribed shares—shares subscribed for by investors but not yet issued to them (usually because of amounts yet to be collected).
6. Unissued shares—shares authorized less issued shares.

D. Types of capital stock:

1. Common stock (may be par or nopar value)—it is the basic stock (has all basic rights including voting right).
2. Preferred stock (may be par or nopar, but usually par)—it is special stock, which is different from the common stock because of preferences. The preferences may be favorable (e.g., cumulative) or unfavorable (nonvoting). The usual "preferences" relate to: (a) dividends, (b) conversion (to common stock) privileges, (c) assets (upon dissolution of the corporation), and (d) voting (or nonvoting).
3. All corporations have common stock. In addition, some also have preferred stock.
4. Nopar stock may be "true" nopar or "stated value." The latter is accounted for in the same way as par value stock.

E. Capital stock, if par value, may be issued at par or at a premium. It is against the laws of most states to issue par value stock at a discount.

1. *Example*: Corporation X is authorized to issue common stock, nopar, and preferred stock, $10 par value per share. 1,000 shares of common were issued at $26 per share and 1,000 shares of preferred were issued at $18 per share. The journal entries for issuance are:

    Common stock:
Cash ($26 × 1,000 shares)	26,000	
Common stock, nopar (1,000 shares)		26,000

    Preferred stock:
Cash ($18 × 1,000 shares)	18,000	
Preferred stock, par $10 (1,000 shares)		10,000
Contributed capital in excess of par, preferred		8,000

2. Nopar stock is recorded in the Common stock account at the total amount received for it. In contrast, the amount received for par value stock is apportioned between two contributed capital accounts. In the above example, the par value of the preferred stock was credited to the Capital stock account, and the premium was credited to a separate contributed capital account.
3. The issue price recorded for capital stock is the cash equivalent amount received (in conformity with the cost principle). This amount includes cash plus the current market value of any other considerations.

F. Treasury stock is a corporation's own capital stock that was sold, collected for, issued, then subsequently reacquired and still held by the corporation. Treasury stock has no voting, dividend, or other stockholder rights.

1. When acquired, the cost of the stock is debited to an account called Treasury stock.

    Example: Company X reacquired 10 shares of its own nopar common stock at $30 per share for cash.

Treasury stock (10 shares)........................	300	
Cash		300

2. Subsequently, five of the shares were sold for $32 per share. The journal entry is:

Cash ($32 × 5 shares)	160	
Treasury stock ($30 × 5 shares)		150
Contributed capital, sale of treasury stock		10

The Treasury stock account has a debit balance and is reported as a negative account (a deduction) in the stockholders' equity section of the balance sheet.

Part B—Accounting for Dividends and Retained Earnings and for Unincorporated Businesses

G. A dividend is a distribution (usually paid in cash) of earnings to the stockholders of the corporation. Therefore, dividends reduce retained earnings and usually reduce cash. However, a dividend may be paid in assets other than cash (this is very infrequent).A cash dividend is recorded on the date it is **declared** by the board of directors of the corporation.

Example: Corporation X has outstanding 10,000 shares of common stock and 5,000 shares of preferred stock. A dividend of $0.50 per share is declared. The journal entry is:

Dividends paid, common stock* (10,000 × $.50)	5,000	
Dividends paid, preferred stock* (5,000 × $.50)	2,500	
Cash (or Dividends payable if the cash is to be paid later)		7,500

    *Closed to Retained earnings, thus, retained earnings is reduced. The Retained earnings account often is debited directly for dividends.

H. Stock dividends may be declared and issued by a corporation. A stock dividend means that the issuing corporation will give the stockholders additional shares of its own stock, rather than cash, as a dividend.

Example: Corporation X has 10,000 shares of common stock outstanding and issues at 1 for 1 stock dividend. The common stock is selling for $15 per share. The journal entry is:

Assume the common stock is nopar:

Retained earnings (10,000 shares × $15)	150,000	
Common stock, nopar (10,000 shares)		150,000

Assume the common stock is par value, $10 per share:

Retained earnings	150,000	
Common stock, par $10 (10,000 shares)		100,000
Contributed capital in excess of par (10,000 shares × $5)		50,000

I. Stock splits are not dividends. They are similar to stock dividends but have a different impact on stockholders' equity. A stock split is accomplished by reducing the par value of the stock. A 2 for 1 stock split would reduce par value per share by 50%.

J. Dividends on preferred stock depend upon the dividend preferences specified in the corporation's charter. Preferred stock may have a single, or a combination, of three dividend preferences.

1. Current dividend preference—This preference specifies that the preferred stockholders must receive their dividends before any dividends are paid to the common stockholders. The current dividend preference almost always is specified as a percent of the par value per share.

Example: Corporation P has capital stock outstanding as follows:

Preferred stock, 6 percent, par $10, 5,000 shares.
Common stock, par $1, 100,000 shares.

A $10,000 cash dividend declared and paid immediately in 19A is recorded as follows:

Dividends paid, preferred (5,000 shares × $10 × 6%)	3,000	
Dividends paid, common (balance)	7,000	
Cash		10,000

2. Cumulative dividend preference—This preference specifies that if the preferred dividend for the current year is not paid (i.e., dividends are passed), the amount not paid cumulates and must be paid in subsequent years before any dividends can be paid on the common shares.

Example: Assume it is 19C for Corporation P (above) and that no dividends were paid in 19A and 19B. A $10,000 dividend declared and paid immediately for 19C is recorded as follows, if the preferred stock is cumulative:

Dividends paid, preferred ($6,000 + $3,000)	9,000	
Dividends in arrears from 19A and 19B:		
(5,000 × $10 × 6% × 2 = $6,000).		
Dividends for 19C: (5,000 × $10 × 6% = $3,000).		
Dividends paid, common (balance)	1,000	
Cash		10,000

K. Prior period adjustments change the beginning balance of retained earnings to correct an error made in an earlier accounting period.

L. Accounting for unincorporated businesses—The fundamentals of accounting and reporting for unincorporated businesses are the same as for a corporation except for the owners' equity. The textbook presents comparative account structures for corporations, partnerships and proprietorships.

12—Questions for Self Evaluation

These questions follow the sequence of the discussions in the chapter. However, they do not cover all of the points discussed in the chapter. After studying the chapter, try to answer each question to the best of your ability without referring again to the chapter. After answering all of them, turn to the solutions in the back and evaluate yourself. This should provide a valuable guide for deciding how much additional study you should commit to the chapter.

1. Both a corporation and a partnership must obtain a charter from the state prior to starting operations.

    _____ T; _____ F

2. The elected governing body of a corporation is called the _____ .

3. The authorized number of shares minus the number of unissued shares equals the number of treasury stock shares. _____ T; _____ F

4. Common and preferred stock may be either par or nopar value. _____ T; _____ F

5. The (a) _____ stock, often called the residual equity, is the "usual or normal" stock, whereas (b) _____ stock has certain special provisions.

6. Par and nopar stock may be sold and issued at a premium, but not at a discount. _____ T; _____ F

7. Match the following:

Definition	*Term*
(a) _____ Number of shares that can be issued	A. Outstanding shares
(b) _____ Number of shares currently owned by investors	B. Treasury stock
	C. Subscribed shares
(c) _____ Shares of own stock reacquired and held by the corporation	D. Authorized shares
	E. Unissued shares
(d) _____ Shares that have been transferred to investors	F. Issued shares
(e) _____ Shares that have never been sold	
(f) _____ Shares sold but not yet issued	

8. From the investors' view, Preferred stock almost always is preferable as an investment.

    _____ T; _____ F

9. Preferred stock usually has one or more of the following four modifications:

   (a) _____

   (b) _____

   (c) _____

   (d) _____

10. _____ preferred stock includes the option to turn in the preferred shares and receive common shares.

11. In accounting for owners' equity, there are no differences between corporations, partnerships, and proprietorships. _____ T; _____ F

12. Briefly define the following:

   (a) Contributed capital: _____

   _____

   (b) Retained earnings: _____

   _____

13. Complete the following stockholders' equity section of the balance sheet:

Stockholders' Equity

   (a) _____ :

   (b) _____ stock, 6 percent, par $10, authorized 5,000 shares,
   issued and outstanding, 1,000 shares . . . . (c) $ _____

   Common stock, nopar, (d) _____ 10,000 shares, issued
   and outstanding, 7,000 shares 140,000
   Contributed capital in excess of par, (e) _____ 6,000
   Total contributed capital . . . . (f) _____

   (g) Retained _____ 30,000

   (h) Total stockholders' equity . . . . $ _____

14. The charter for Corporation X authorized 10,000 shares of $10 par value preferred stock and 20,000 shares of nopar common stock. The corporation sold and issued 500 shares of preferred stock at $16 per share and 10,000 shares of common stock at $22 per share. Give the journal entries indicated (if none explain why).

   (a) At date of authorization:

   _____ _____ _____

   _____ _____ _____

   _____ _____ _____

   _____ _____ _____

   _____ _____ _____

(b) At date of sale and issuance:

_____   _____   _____
_____   _____   _____
_____   _____   _____
_____   _____   _____
_____   _____   _____
_____   _____   _____
_____   _____   _____
_____   _____   _____

15. Because the Treasury stock account has a debit balance, it often is referred to as a _____
_____ account.

16. When treasury stock is purchased for cash, the _____ account and _____
are reduced by equal amounts.

17. Adams Corporation has 4,000 shares of its $10 par value common stock outstanding (originally sold at $12 per share). The corporation purchased the 100 shares held by one individual for $18 per share and paid cash.

(a) Give the journal entry for the treasury stock.

_____   _____   _____
_____   _____   _____
_____   _____   _____

(b) Two years later half of the treasury stock was sold at $25 per share (cash). Give the required journal entry.

_____   _____   _____
_____   _____   _____
_____   _____   _____
_____   _____   _____

(c) Complete the following stockholders' equity section of the balance sheet after the above entries:

Stockholders' Equity

Contributed Capital:
Common stock, par $10, authorized 5,000 shares, issued 4,000 shares, of which
(1) _____ shares are held as (2) _____ .... (3) $ _____
Contributed capital in excess of par .... (4) _____
(5) Total contributed capital ....
Retained earnings   25,000
(6) Less ....
(7) Total stockholders' equity $ _____

157

18. At December 31, 19B, end of the annual accounting period, Blount Corporation showed the following items in the post-closing trial balance:

Common stock, par $10 (10,000 shares authorized)	$70,000
Retained earnings.......................................	25,000
Treasury stock (100 shares)	(1,700)
Contributed capital in excess of par.....................	21,000

Prepare the stockholders' equity section of the balance sheet.

Stockholders' Equity

_____ :

_____

_____

_____

_____

_____

_____

_____

_____

_____

_____

_____

19. When an investor purchases stock in a corporation as an investment, future cash inflows are expected from two sources. They are:

(a) _____

(b) _____

20. In order to pay a cash dividend a corporation must have sufficient:

(a) _____

(b) _____

21. When a cash dividend is paid, the effect on the corporation is to decrease _____

and _____ .

22. When treasury stock is purchased, the effect on the corporation is to decrease _____

and _____ .

23. If preferred stock is _____ , any dividends on it not paid in a given year are lost by the preferred stockholders.

24. Preferred stock may carry three kinds of dividend preferences; two of them are:

   A. Current dividend preference
   B. Cumulative dividend preference

   Each of these is defined below. You are to match them by entering the appropriate code letter to the left.

   (a) _____ If all or part of the specified preferred dividend is not paid in a given year, the dividends not paid must be given priority over common stock dividends.

   (b) _____ The preferred stock may share proportionately with the common stock in all dividends paid.

25. Baker Corporation has the following capital stock outstanding:

   5% preferred stock, par $10, 5,000 shares
   Common stock, par $2, 20,000 shares

   Complete the tabulation below for each separate case to show the amount of dividends that would be paid to the preferred and common stockholders respectively:

Cases	Dividends Paid to Stockholders		
	Preferred	Common	Total
A—Preferred is noncumulative; nonparticipating; total dividends paid, $2,500.			
B—Preferred is same as in A; total dividends paid, $6,000.			
C—Preferred is cumulative; nonparticipating; no dividends were paid during prior two years; total dividends paid, $14,900.			

26. When a stock dividend is distributed, capital stock _____ increases or _____ decreases and retained earnings _____ increases or _____ decreases.

27. The transfer of retained earnings to contributed capital because of a stock dividend is called _____ retained earnings.

28. Blue Corporation has outstanding 10,000 shares of common stock, par $20 per share. The stock currently is selling for $35 per share. A stock dividend is declared whereby each stockholder will receive one additional share of common stock for each 10 shares now held. Give the journal entry to record this stock dividend.

_____ _____ _____

_____ _____ _____

_____ _____ _____

_____ _____ _____

159

29. A corporation has 10,000 shares of common stock, par $30, outstanding.

(a) Assume a three-for-one stock dividend (i.e., for each share held, three additional shares are issued). The par value per share after the distribution would be $_____ per share and the number of shares outstanding would be _____.

(b) Assume instead that there was a three-for-one stock split (i.e., each share is called in, and in its place three new shares are issued). The par value per share after the distribution would be $_____, and the number of shares outstanding would be _____.

30. Complete the following:

A stock split causes the amount of:	Enter Appropriate Checks		
	Increase	Decrease	No Effect
(a) Assets to....................................	_____	_____	_____
(b) Liabilities to	_____	_____	_____
(c) Contributed capital to	_____	_____	_____
(d) Retained earnings to	_____	_____	_____
(e) Total owners' equity to......................	_____	_____	_____
(f) Number of outstanding shares to	_____	_____	_____
(g) Par value per share to	_____	_____	_____

31. When a cash dividend is declared at one date and paid at a later date, a liability is recorded on the (a) _____ date, the liability is paid on the (b) _____ date, and no accounting entry is made on the (c) _____ date.

32. Complete the following by providing the appropriate titles:

Description	Title
(a) The record maintained by the corporation that shows the name, address, and number of shares owned by each stockholder	_____
(b) An outside agent often hired to maintain the records on each stockholder that shows all stock transfers (sales and acquisitions)	_____
(c) Official record of the actions of all meetings of the board of directors and stockholders	_____

33. Complete the following statement by filling in the lettered blanks:

CORPORATION W
Statement of Retained Earnings

(a) _____ December 31, 19D

Retained earnings balance, January 1, 19D.............................	$150,000
(b) _____:	
Correction of accounting error (after tax)	10,000
(c) _____	140,000
(d) _____	25,000
Total	165,000
(e) Deduct _____:	
(f) on _____ $15,000	
(g) on common _____	20,000
(h) _____	$

34. Match each of the following accounting terms with its proper definition by inserting the letter which identifies the definition in the space next to the term.

Accounting Terms

_____ (1) Authorized shares

_____ (2) Charter of a corporation

_____ (3) Common stock

_____ (4) Convertible preferred stock

_____ (5) Cumulative dividend preference

_____ (6) Current dividend preference

_____ (7) Dividend dates: Declaration

_____ (8) Record

_____ (9) Payment

_____ (10) Dividends in arrears

_____ (11) Issued shares

_____ (12) Legal or stated capital

_____ (13) Minute book

_____ (14) Nopar value stock

_____ (15) Outstanding shares

_____ (16) Par value

_____ (17) Partnership

_____ (18) Preferred stock

_____ (19) Prior period adjustments

_____ (20) Restrictions on retained earnings

_____ (21) Sole proprietorship

_____ (22) Stock certificate

_____ (23) Stock dividends

_____ (24) Stock splits

_____ (25) Stock transfer agent

_____ (26) Stockholders' subsidiary ledger

_____ (27) Treasury stock

_____ (28) Unissued shares

Definitions

A. Shares of stock, in total, that are owned by stockholders on any particular date

B. Shares of a corporation's stock that have never been issued

C. Date dividend declared; entry for dividends payable

D. The total number of authorized shares are increased by a specified ratio; issued at no cost; does not change proportional ownership of each stockholder

E. An official record of the actions of the board of directors of a corporation

F. Preferred stock preference that dividends not declared for a particular year cumulate as a subsequent preference

G. Dividends on cumulative preferred stock that have not been declared in prior years

H. An unincorporated business owned by only one person (one owner)

I. Maximum number of shares of the corporation that can be issued as specified in the charter

J. Evidence of the number of shares of stock held by an investor; ownership interest

K. Total shares of stock that have been issued; shares outstanding plus treasury shares held

L. An unincorporated business owned by two or more persons

M. Distribution of additional shares of stock to current stockholders on a proportional basis at no cost

N. Preferred stock that is convertible at the option of the holder, to common stock

O. Shares of stock that have specified rights over the common stock

P. The dividend preference on preferred stock for a particular year

Q. Shares of capital stock that have no par value specified in the corporate charter

R. A record, usually maintained by a stock transfer agent, of the names, addresses, and shares owned, of all of the stockholders

S. Amounts debited or credited directly to retained earnings resulting from correction of accounting errors

T. The legal articles of incorporation by the state that creates a corporation; specifies purpose and capital

U. An individual or organization appointed by a corporation to transfer shares and maintain stockholders' records

V. Date on which a cash dividend is paid to the stockholders of record; cash is disbursed

W. The basic, normal, voting stock issued by a corporation; not preferred stock; residual equity

X. Temporary removal of some or all of the balance of retained earnings from dividend availability

Y. Nominal value per share of capital stock; specified in the charter; basis for legal capital

Z. Defined by state law; usually par value; provides a "cushion" for creditors; cannot be used for dividends

AA. Date on which the stockholders are individually identifed to receive a declared dividend

BB. A corporation's own stock that has been issued then reacquired and held by that corporation

13

Measuring and Reporting Long-Term Investments

PURPOSE OF THIS CHAPTER

One corporation may invest in the capital stock of another corporation for a variety of reasons. Often the investment is for a short term, designed to earn a return on idle funds. Accounting for short-term investments was discussed in Chapter 8. Some investments in the stock of other corporations are for the long term. These investments may be designed to provide the investing corporation with significant influence or control over the other corporation. Long-term investments that do not provide the investor with control are discussed in this chapter. Long-term investments that provide control are discussed in Chapter 14. This chapter also discusses investments in the bonds of another corporation. These investments always are designed to provide a return on idle funds because bond investments never provide the investor with the ability to influence the other corporation (i.e., bonds do not have voting rights).

HOW TO STUDY THIS CHAPTER

This chapter discusses long-term investments in the capital stock of another company (Part A) and in the bonds of another entity (Part B). You should review Chapters 8 (Short-Term Investments) and 11 (Bonds Payable). This chapter is somewhat complex because of the different methods of accounting used for investments in capital stock. Part B, bond investments, involves the concepts of measurement and amortization of discount and premium. These discussions parallel those in Chapter 11 for bonds payable, except that investments relate to the other party in the transactions. You should study the two parts of this chapter as essentially separate topics because some different concepts are used. Careful study of the explanations and the illustrations is essential. The Demonstration Case should be studied because it ties together investments in stocks and bonds. You must attain a good understanding of Part A as a foundation for Chapter 14 (consolidated statements).

STUDY OUTLINE OF THIS CHAPTER

Part A—Long-Term Investments in Equity Securities (Stocks)

A. Short-term investments (defined in Chapter 8) meet the twofold test of (1) ready marketability and (2) management intention to convert them to cash in the short run. They are reported as current assets. Investments not meeting the twofold test are known as long-term investments and are reported on the balance sheet under a noncurrent caption called "Investments and Funds," or simply, "Long-Term Investments."

1. A long-term investment may be in the capital stock (equity securities) or bonds (debt securities) of another company, or in other assets (such as land held for investment purposes).

B. Accounting for a long-term investment in the stock of another corporation depends upon the type of stock and the level of stock ownership; that is, the percent of shares owned of the voting common stock outstanding of the other company. The levels of ownership and the accounting approaches may be outlined as follows:

Level of Ownership	Proportion of Voting Shares Owned	Accounting Approach
Neither significant influence nor control	Less than 20% of the outstanding shares	Cost method
Significant influence but not control	20% or more, but not more than 50% of the outstanding shares	Equity method
Control (Discussed in Chapter 14)	Over 50% of the outstanding shares	Consolidated statement method

1. All proportions of nonvoting stock are accounted for under the cost method.

C. When the cost method (less than 20 percent ownership of the outstanding voting shares) is used, the long-term investment is recorded at its cash equivalent cost at date of acquisition.

Example: Company A purchased 10 percent of the 10,000 shares of outstanding common shares (voting) of Company B at $22.50 per share. The journal entry to record the acquisition is:

Long-term investment, stock of Company B
 (1,000 shares)   22,500
  Cash (1,000 shares × $22.50)   22,500

1. Subsequent to acquisition, dividends received on the stock investment are recorded as investment revenue.

    Example: Company B declared and paid a cash dividend of $1.50 per share. Company A would record this dividend as follows:

    Cash (1,000 shares × $1.50)* 1,500
        Revenue from investments 1,500

    *A debit to dividends receivable would be made if the dividends were
    declared but not paid.

2. Subsequent to acquisition, a long-term investment in equity securities (i.e., capital stock) of another company when accounted for under the cost method must be carried at the **lower-of-cost-or-market (LCM)**. Lower-of-cost-or-market is applied to the total equity portfolio.

    (a) When the investment portfolio is written down to market (when market is lower) an unrealized loss is recorded (a debit) and reported as a separate deduction in owners' equity. The offsetting credit is to an allowance account (a contra account to the investment account). The recording of an unrealized loss on long-term investments does not affect net income.

    (b) If the market recovers (after the portfolio previously has been written down below cost), the unrealized loss is "reversed" so that the investment account is at cost or market (if still below cost). The investment account is **never** increased above cost.

    (c) Illustration of cost method:

    (1) January 1, 19A, X Company purchased the following equity securities:

    AB Corporation common stock, 2,000 shares (nopar) at $50 per share (outstanding shares, 40,000)
    CD Corporation preferred stock, 1,000 shares (par $10) nonvoting at $30 per share (outstanding shares, 6,000)

    Journal entry by X Company:

    Long-term investments 130,000
        Cash 130,000
        (2,000 × $50) + (1,000 × $30) = $130,000

167

(2) During December, 19A, AB Corporation declared and paid a cash dividend of $1 per share. X Company would record the dividend as follows:

Cash (2,000 × $1)	2,000	
Investment revenue....................		2,000

(3) December 31, 19A, end of the accounting period, the quoted market prices were:

AB Corporation common	$45
CD Corporation preferred	31

Journal entry by X Company:

Unrealized loss on long-term investments	9,000	
Allowance to reduce long-term investments to LCM		9,000

Computation:

Stock	Cost	Market on Dec. 31, 19A
AB Common ...	2,000 × $50 = $100,000	2,000 × $45 = $ 90,000
CD Preferred...	1,000 × $30 = 30,000	1,000 × $31 = 31,000
	$130,000	$121,000

Balance required in the allowance account:
$130,000 − $121,000 = $9,000

(4) Financial statement amounts for 19A:

Income Statement

Investment revenue..	$ 2,000

Balance Sheet

Assets:

Long-term investments................................	$130,000	
Less: Allowance to reduce to LCM..................	9,000	$121,000

Stockholders' Equity:

Contributed capital....................................	x,xxx
Retained earnings	x,xxx
Unrealized loss on long-term investments	($9,000)

(5) December 31, 19B, end of the accounting period, the quoted market prices were:

AB Corporation common	$52
CD Corporation preferred	30

Journal entry by X Company:

Allowance to reduce long-term investments to LCM	9,000	
Unrealized loss on long-term investments (i.e., loss recovered)		9,000

Computations:

Stock	Cost	Market on Dec. 31, 19A
AB Common ...	2,000 × $50 = $100,000	2,000 × $52 = $104,000
CD Preferred...	1,000 × $30 = 30,000	1,000 × $30 = 30,000
	$130,000	$134,000

Balance required in the allowance account:
  None, because total market is greater than total cost.
  Report the investments at cost because the investment account cannot be increased above cost.

D. When the **equity method** (20 percent or more ownership of the voting shares, but not over 50 percent) is used, the **acquisition** of the investment is recorded at cost (exactly the same as for the cost method). However, **subsequent to acquisition**, the investor's proportionate share of the reported net income of the other company is recognized as investment revenue under the equity method. Because the income of the other company is recognized as revenue, any dividends received out of that income cannot be recognized as revenue because that would amount to double counting. Any dividends received must be credited to the investment account.

1. Illustration of the equity method:

(a) Company R purchased 30 percent of the 20,000 shares of outstanding common stock of Company S for $40 per share. The acquisition is recorded at cost as follows:

Long-term investment, stock of Company S (6,000 shares × $40)...................	240,000	
Cash...............................		240,000

(b) Subsequently, Company S reported net income for the year of $15,000. Company R would recognize its proportionate interest as investment revenue:

Long-term investment, stock of Company S	4,500	
Revenue from investments ($15,000 × 30% = $4,500)		4,500

(c) Company S declared and paid a cash dividend of $.50 per share. Company R would record the dividend as follows:

Cash (6,000 shares × $.50)	3,000	
Long-term investment, stock of Company S		3,000

Note that investment revenue is not affected by the dividend when the equity method is used

2. When the **equity method** is used, long-term investments are reported on the balance sheet at the amount shown in the investment account; and the investment revenue is reported on the income statement. Also, both acquisition cost and market should be disclosed. LCM is not used with the equity method

Example: The long-term investment held by Company R (above) is reported as follows:

Balance Sheet

Investments and Funds:
  Investment in common stock, Company S, equity basis (cost, $240,000; market, $235,000) $241,500

Income Statement

Revenue from investments....................................... $ 4,500

Part B—Long-Term Investments in Debt Securities (Bonds)

E. Bonds are acquired as a long-term investment because they offer the advantages of a fixed (stated) interest rate and return of the principal at maturity date.

1. Bond investments may be acquired at **par**, at a **discount**, or at a **premium**. The cash equivalent cost at acquisition date is debited to the investment account.

Example: Company X purchased $10,000 of the 6 percent bonds of Company Y for cash. The bonds pay interest semiannually (3%) and mature in five years from date of acquisition. The acquisition is recorded as follows, assuming acquisition on an interest date:

	Assuming the Bonds Were Acquired at—		
	Par	*A Discount*	*A Premium*
Long-term investment, 6% bonds, Company Y	10,000	9,700	10,300
Cash....................	10,000	9,700	10,300

170

2. Interest collected on each interest date is recorded as investment revenue, and any discount or premium is amortized over the **remaining life** (i.e., acquisition to maturity dates) of the bonds.

Example: The interest received on the first interest date on the above bonds is recorded as follows on the semiannual interest date, assuming straight-line amortization:

	Assuming the Bonds Were Acquired at—				
	Par		A Discount		A Premium
Cash ($10,000 × 3%).........	300		300		300
Long-term investment, bonds*			30		30
Revenue from investments		300		330	270

*$300 × 1/10 = $30 amortization each semiannual period for five years.

Notice that the premium and discount were not recorded in separate accounts. Therefore, the amortization entry was made directly to the investment account. Separate premium and discount accounts could have been used with the same end results.

F. When an investment is disposed of (i.e., sold), the amount in the investment account for that investment must be removed.

Example: Assume the above bond investment was sold after the second year for $10,100. The journal entry is recorded as follows, assuming straight-line amortization:

	Assuming the Bonds Were Acquired at—				
	Par		A Discount		A Premium
Cash....................	10,100		10,100		10,100
Long-term investment* ...		10,000		9,820	10,180
Gain on sale of investment		100		280	
Loss on sale of investment.....					80

*The amount in the investment account after four semiannual periods would be:

Discount: $ 9,700 + $120 = $ 9,820
Premium: $10,300 − $120 = $10,180

G. Bond investments purchased (or sold) between interest dates require recognition of accrued interest from the last interest date to date of purchase (or sale).

1. Recognition of accrued interest is necessary because (a) the purchaser receives the full amount of interest at the next interest date, but (b) the seller is entitled to interest for that part of the period held before sale. Therefore, upon sale, the seller collects the sales price plus the accrued interest.

   Example: On November 1, 19A, Company A purchased a $1,000, 6 percent bond of Company B as a long-term investment. The bond interest is paid semiannually (3%) on June 30 and December 31. The purchase price was par plus the accrued interest. Each company would record this transaction as follows on November 1, 19A:

   Company A—Investor:

Long-term investment, bond	1,000	
Investment (interest) revenue ($1,000 × 6% × 4/12)...	20	
Cash $1,000 + ($1,000 × 6% × 4/12)		1,020

   Company B—Issuer (seller):

Cash...	1,020	
Interest expense................................		20
Bonds payable		1,000

H. Effective-Interest Amortization—A premium or discount associated with a bond investment may be amortized using the effective-interest approach (which was discussed in Chapter 11). Exhibit 13-5 in the textbook presents a schedule which may be used to calculate effective-interest amortization.

13—Questions for Self Evaluation

These questions follow the sequence of the discussions in the chapter. However, they do not cover all of the points discussed in the chapter. After studying the chapter, try to answer each question to the best of your ability without referring again to the chapter. After answering all of them, turn to the solutions in the back and evaluate yourself. This should provide a valuable guide for deciding how much additional study you should commit to the chapter.

1. If an investment is made with the purpose of ultimately exercising significant influence or control, the security will be _____. Alternatively, if the purpose is to receive revenue regardless of the periodic net income, the security will be _____.

2. At acquisition, long-term investments are accounted for in conformity with the _____ _____ principle.

3. The cost of a long term investment in debt securities should be recorded at the purchase price plus any accrued interest between the purchase and last interest dates. _____ T; _____ F

4. Match the following in respect to accounting for a long-term investment in equity securities:

   (a) _____ Neither significant influence nor control   A.   Equity method

   (b) _____ Control   B.   Cost method

   (c) _____ Significant influence but not control   C.   Consolidated statement
                                                                        method

5. Match the following in respect to accounting for a long-term investment in equity securities (common voting stock):

   (a) _____ Over 50 percent of the outstanding shares   A.   Significant influence
                                                                        but not control

   (b) _____ Less than 20 percent of the outstanding shares   B.   Neither significant
                                                                        influence nor control.

   (c) _____ 20 percent or more, but not more than 50 percent   C.   Control
              of the outstanding shares

6. Accounting for long-term investments depends on whether the investor has:

   (a) Significant influence, which is defined as _____

   _____

   _____

(b) Control, which is defined as _____

_____

_____

_____

(c) Neither significant influence nor control.

7. In respect to long-term investments in equity securities:

   (a) Where there is neither significant influence nor control the _____ method must be used.

   (b) When there is significant influence but not control the _____ method must be used.

   (c) When there is control the _____ method must be used.

8. Under the cost method the investing company recognizes revenue from the investee company when the:

   A. Investee company publishes its financial statements.
   B. Investee company reports net income.
   C. Investor company declares a cash dividend.
   D. Investee company declares a cash dividend.
   E. None of the above.

9. Under the equity method the investing company recognizes revenue from the investee company when the:

   A. Investor company reports net income.
   B. Investee company reports net income.
   C. Investor company declares a cash dividend.
   D. Investee company declares a cash dividend.
   E. None of the above.

10. On January 1, 19D, Corporation A purchased some of the 30,000 shares of common stock outstanding of Corporation B. At the end of 19D, Corporation B reported net income of $20,000, paid cash dividends of $10,000 and the market price at the end of 19D was $24 per share. Give the journal entries for Corporation A for each case. If no entry, so state.

Case A—Purchased 3,000 shares at $25 per share:

   (a) At acquisition:

   _____   _____ _____

   _____   _____ _____

   _____   _____ _____

   (b) Reported earnings of Corporation B:

   _____   _____ _____

   _____   _____ _____

   _____   _____ _____

174

(c) Dividends declared and paid by Corporation B:

_____   _____   _____

_____   _____   _____

_____   _____   _____

(d) Market price at end 19D:

_____   _____   _____

_____   _____   _____

_____   _____   _____

Case B—Purchased 9,000 shares at $25 per share:

(a) At acquisition:

_____   _____   _____

_____   _____   _____

_____   _____   _____

(b) Reported earnings of Corporation B:

_____   _____   _____

_____   _____   _____

_____   _____   _____

(c) Dividends declared and paid by Corporation B:

_____   _____   _____

_____   _____   _____

_____   _____   _____

(d) Market price at end 19D:

_____   _____   _____

_____   _____   _____

_____   _____   _____

11. Under the cost method of accounting for long-term investments in equity securities, LCM must be applied when the market value of the portfolio falls below cost. _____ T; _____F

12, All nonvoting stock owned as a long-term investment must be accounted for under the cost method regardless of the number of shares held. _____ T; _____ F

13. On December 31, 19B (the end of the accounting period), Company T owned the following long-term investments which are accounted for under the cost method.

Corporation	Type of Stock	Number of Shares	Cost per Share	Market Value Dec. 31, 19B
A	Common, nopar	1,000	$15	$16
B	Preferred, par $10	2,000	20	15
C	Common, par $1	3,000	10	11

(a) The dollar value that should be reported on the 19B balance sheet for long-term investments is:

    A. $85,000.
    B. $79,000.
    C. $75,000.
    D. None of the above; it is $ _____ .

(b) The 19B income statement should report an "unrealized" loss on the investment of:

    A. $10,000.
    B. $6,000.
    C. zero amount.
    D. None of the above; it is $ _____ .

(c) The account "Allowance to reduce long-term investments to LCM" should reflect (on the 19B balance sheet):

    A. $85,000.
    B. $75,000.
    C. $10,000.
    D. $6,000.
    E. None of the above; it is $ _____ .

(d) The "Allowance" account in C above should be reported on the 19B balance sheet as:

    A. Debit under assets.
    B. Contra account under stockholders' equity.
    C. Contra account under assets.
    D. None of the above, it is _____ .

14. In accounting for long-term investments under the equity method, LCM is not applied. _____ T; _____ F

15. Under the equity method, the investor company recognizes revenue from the investee company when cash dividends are received. _____ T; _____ F

16. In contrast to capital stock, a long-term investment in bonds provides a specified cash inflow for:

(a) _____ and (b) _____ .

17. A long-term investment in both capital stock and bonds confers voting privileges to the investor. _____ T; _____ F

18. A $1,000, 10 percent bond of Company A is purchased as a long-term investment by Company B. Interest is payable each six months. How much interest revenue will be collected in cash by the investor on each interest date assuming the bond is purchased at:

(a) par (100) $_____; (b) discount (95) $_____; (c) premium (105) $_____?

19. The amount of revenue that should be recognized on a long-term investment in bonds purchased at a premium is the interest received plus interest revenue accrued and minus an appropriate amortization amount of the premium. _____ T; _____ F

20. Company A owns a $10,000, 9 percent bond investment (acquired at par) and the annual interest date is August 31. If the annual accounting period for Company A ends on December 31, how much interest must be accrued? $_____.

21. A $5,000, 12 percent bond is purchased at 104 as a long-term investment four years before maturity date. Assume straight-line amortization. What would be the debit balance in the long-term investment account:

(a) At the date of acquisition? $_____.

(b) At the end of the first year? $_____.

(c) On the maturity date? $_____.

22. A bond is purchased at a discount as a long-term investment. Amortization of the discount will increase the amount of revenue from investment. _____ T; _____ F

23. A $1,000, 10 percent bond is purchased as an investment for $1,070, seven years before the maturity date. The interest is payable annually. Assume straight-line amortization.

(a) What amount should be debited to the investment account at date of acquisition?

$_____.

(b) How much cash will be collected each year as interest on the investment?

$_____.

(c) What will be the net cash earned on this investment over the seven years?

$_____.

(d) How much investment revenue will be reported on the income statement each year?

$_____.

24. On September 1, 19B, Company P purchased as a long-term investment a $3,000, 10 percent bond of Company S at par plus accrued interest. Interest is payable each June 30. Give the journal entry to record this acquisition.

_____ _____ _____

_____ _____ _____

_____ _____ _____

_____ _____ _____

25. On September 1, 19B, Company P purchased as a long-term investment a $2,000, 9 percent bond of Company T at 102 plus accrued interest. Interest is payable each June 30. Give the journal entry to record this acquisition.

_____   _____   _____
_____   _____   _____
_____   _____   _____
_____   _____   _____

26. Company A purchased as a long-term investment a $1,000, 10 percent bond of another company at $1,050 on January 1, 19A. The bond matures on December 31, 19E. Interest is paid each June 30 and December 31, and straight-line amortization is used. On January 1, 19D, Company A sold the bond for $1,000 cash. Give the journal entry to record the disposition of the investment.

_____   _____   _____
_____   _____   _____
_____   _____   _____
_____   _____   _____

27. Match each of the following accounting terms with its proper definition by inserting the letter which identifies the definition in the space next to the term.

Accounting Terms	Definitions
_____ (1) Control	A. Method used if investor owns less than 20 percent of the voting stock of the investor company
_____ (2) Cost method	B. Method used if investor owns 20-50 percent of the voting stock of the investor company
_____ (3) Discount	C. The annual rate of cash interest specified in the bond contract
_____ (4) Equity method	D. The ability of an investor to determine the operating and financing policies of another company
_____ (5) Premium	E. The ability of an investor to have an important impact on the operating and financing policies of another company
_____ (6) Significant influence	F. A bond that is purchased for more than par value is purchased at a premium
_____ (7) Stated interest rate	G. A bond that is purchased for less than par value is purchased at a discount

14

Consolidated Statements—
Measuring and Reporting

PURPOSE OF THIS CHAPTER

The previous chapter discussed accounting for long-term investments when one corporation owns less than 50 percent of the voting stock of another corporation. This chapter discusses those situations in which one corporation has a controlling influence over another corporation as the result of owning more than 50 percent of the outstanding voting stock of the other corporation. Often, when a corporation has a controlling influence in another corporation, the financial statements for each corporation are combined into a single set of financial statements by an accounting process called consolidation. Because most large companies prepare consolidated financial statements, an understanding of the consolidation process is important for both accounting majors and anyone who uses financial statements.

HOW TO STUDY THIS CHAPTER

This chapter introduces the concepts underlying consolidated financial statements. The concepts are not difficult to comprehend. A careful reading of the chapter with reasonable attention to the illustrations and the assigned homework should provide you with the requisite level of knowledge for understanding consolidated statements. Often an advanced accounting course is taught that devotes most of a semester or term just to the subject of consolidated financial statements. In studying this chapter, you should keep the broad concepts in mind, and, in addition, focus on understanding the fundamental distinctions between combinations by pooling of interests and by purchase.

STUDY OUTLINE OF THIS CHAPTER

Part A—Acquiring a Controlling Interest

A. When one company owns over 50 percent of the outstanding common stock (voting stock) of another corporation, control is presumed to exist. The investing company is known as the **parent** company, and the other corporation is called a **subsidiary**. Both corporations continue as separate legal entities.

1. When control is present, the financial statements of the parent and the subsidiaries must be prepared and then combined into **consolidated financial statements**.

2. Consolidated financial statements must be prepared **by the parent** (but not by the subsidiary) in every case where control exists. Certain foreign subsidiaries are not consolidated if government regulations prevent the parent company from exercising meaningful control of the subsidiary.

B. One corporation may obtain control of another corporation by:

1. Organizing a new corporation and retaining more than 50 percent of the **voting** common stock of the new corporation.

2. Acquiring more than 50 percent of the **voting** common stock of an already existing corporation. Basically, the acquisition may be done in either of two ways as follows:

    (a) A pooling of interests—This occurs when the shares of the parent are exchanged for shares of the subsidiary (and the exchange meets each of the requirements set forth in APB Opinion No. 16).
    (b) Purchase—This occurs when the shares of the subsidiary are purchased by the parent with cash, other assets, or debt.

C. Pooling of interests (a book value approach)—Because this kind of acquisition involves the exchange of shares (and no payment of assets), it is not viewed as a purchase/sale transaction. Therefore, the consolidated financial statements are on a strictly book value basis. The amounts on the financial statements of the subsidiary are added to those of the parent, on a line-by-line basis, without any change in their value. Thus, the book values reported by the subsidiary are added to the book values of the parent to derive the consolidated statements.

1. This book value accounting approach is used because under the pooling of interests method, the exchange of shares for shares is not deemed to be an exchange transaction but only a swap of "paper." Therefore, the cost principle does not apply.

2. In combining the financial statements of the parent and the subsidiary into one by the parent company, all **intercompany items are eliminated**. These items include intercompany debt, intercompany revenue, the investment account on the books of the parent, and certain owners' equity accounts of the subsidiary.

3. Combination of two or more sets of financial statements into one consolidated set usually is accomplished on a special worksheet to facilitate the work. The accounts (accounting records) of neither company are affected by the consolidation process because it simply is the "adding together" of the separate financial statements of the parent and its subsidiaries.

D. Purchase (a market value approach)—Because this kind of acquisition involves actual purchase of more than 50 percent of the voting common shares of the other corporation, a completed purchase-sale transaction is deemed to have occurred. Therefore, the cost principle is applicable.

1. The values of the assets of the subsidiary are changed from their book value, as reported by the subsidiary, to their current **market values at date of acquisition**, for consolidation purposes. This means that the market values of the assets of the subsidiary (rather than the "book" values it reports on its financial statements) are added to the book values reported on the financial statements of the parent.

2. This approach often causes an asset called "goodwill" to appear on the consolidated financial statements (which is not true of the pooling of interests method).

181

E. Illustration of the pooling of interests method of preparing consolidated financial statements immediately after acquisition (i.e. book values + book values):

   1. Pooling of interests—Refer to the preacquisition data given in the textbook, Exhibit 14-1 for the parent (Company P) and the subsidiary (Company S).

   2. Study Exhibit 14-3 of the textbook to learn how the two financial statements are combined into one consolidated statement (of the parent company). Particularly study (a) the eliminations and (b) how the book values of the two companies were combined (i.e., consolidated) in the last column.

F. Illustration of the purchase method of preparing consolidated financial statements immediately after acquisition (i.e., book values + market values):

   1. Refer to Exhibits 14-1 in the textbook for background illustrative data.

   2. Study Exhibit 14-4 and give particular attention to (a) the eliminations, (b) goodwill, and (c) how the market values of the subsidiary company are added to the book values of the parent company. Also, study the computation of goodwill ($10,000).

Part B—Reporting Consolidated Operations after Acquisition

G. For accounting periods **subsequent** to acquisition, the required financial statements are consolidated by the parent company following the same concepts outlined above for (a) pooling of interests and (b) purchase.

   1. Any goodwill recognized at acquisition (i.e., only under the purchase method) must be amortized over its estimated "useful" life, but not to exceed 40 years, (APB Opinion No. 17).

2. Any increase in the value of property, plant and equipment recorded at acquisition (i.e., only under the purchase method) must be depreciated over the remaining life of the asset.

3. Eliminations of intercompany transactions are made in each year subsequent to acquisition in the same manner as shown in Part A at acquisition.

H. Exhibits 14–6 (pooling of interests) and 14–7 (purchase) show consolidation worksheets subsequent to acquisition.

14—Questions for Self Evaluation

These questions follow the sequence of the discussions in the chapter. However, they do not cover all of the points discussed in the chapter. After studying the chapter, try to answer each question to the best of your ability without referring again to the chapter. After answering all of them, turn to the solutions in the back and evaluate yourself. This should provide a valuable guide for deciding how much additional study you should commit to the chapter.

1. Consolidated financial statements are prepared to include all subsidiaries of which the parent company owns more than 50 percent of the voting common stock. _____ T; _____ F

2. Both the parent and its subsidiary companies prepare consolidated financial statements. _____ T; _____ F

3. A subsidiary prepares and uses its own separate financial statements rather than the consolidated financial statements which include the parent's accounts. _____ T; _____ F

4. When a company owns over 50 percent of the outstanding voting stock of another company, and qualifies for consolidation, both the accounting and reporting are affected for both companies. _____ T; _____ F

5. Consolidated statements usually must be prepared by the parent company when (a) _____ _____ of the common stock is owned. In this situation a (b) _____ _____ relationship is said to exist.

6. In situations where consolidated financial statements are to be prepared (by the parent company), each company prepares its own separate financial statements, then _____ _____ .

7. Control is presumed to exist when _____ .

8. Because the consolidated financial statement approach does not affect the recording of transactions in the accounts of either corporation, it relates only to the _____ of financial results.

9. The cost principle is not applicable in accounting for a pooling of interests. _____ T; _____ F

10. When the parent acquires a controlling interest in the common stock of another corporation by exchanging stock for stock, it is usually a (a) _____ ; in all other situations it is a (b) _____ .

11. Goodwill usually must be recognized in a pooling of interests. _____ T; _____ F

12. Corporation X acquired 90 percent of the voting common shares of Corporation Y by exchanging its own shares on a 2 to 1 basis. This is called a _____ .

13. In preparing consolidated statements under a pooling of interests the book values of the subsidiary company are added to the _____ values of the parent company.

14. Company P is negotiating to acquire 90 percent of the voting common shares of Company S (from the stockholders of Company S) under one of two alternative approaches. Match the journal entries for acquisition given below for Company P with the accounting method.

Journal Entries	*Method*
_____ (1) Investment in stock of Co. S .... 220,000 Cash 220,000	(A) Pooling of interests (B) Purchase
_____ (2) Investment in stock of Co. S .... 200,000 Common stock .... 150,000 Contributed capital in excess of par 50,000	(C) None of the above
_____ (3) Investment in bonds of Co. S .... 200,000 Cash 200,000	

15. A consolidated set of financial statements views the parent and subsidiary as a single economic entity.

_____ T; _____ F

16. In preparing the consolidated financial statements of Company P and Company S, the parent company made the following elimination:

    Receivable from Company S (decrease) $1,000
    Payable to Company P (decrease) 1,000

This elimination represents an _____ .

17. Company S had 10,000 shares of $20 par value common stock outstanding and retained earnings of $40,000. Company P acquired all of these shares.

(a) Company P purchased the shares for cash at $30 per share. This is called a _____

    _____ .

Journal entry by Company P:

_____   _____ _____

_____   _____ _____

_____   _____ _____

_____   _____ _____

(b) Company P acquired the shares of Company S by exchange of two of its own common shares, par $5, for each share of the stock of Company S. This is called a _____ .

Journal entry by Company P:

_____   _____ _____

_____   _____ _____

_____   _____ _____

_____   _____ _____

18. In consolidated financial statements under the purchase method the _____ values of the subsidiary company are added to the _____ values of the parent company.

19. For the same set of basic data about the parent and subsidiary companies, the pooling of interests and purchase methods produce approximately the same consolidated financial statement amounts.

_____ T; _____ F

20. When preparing a consolidated balance sheet, all debts and receivables between the parent and subsidiary must be eliminated. Elimination entries are necessary because _____

_____

_____

_____

_____

21. In preparing a consolidated balance sheet, goodwill normally arises when the combination is by

(a) _____ , but never arises when the combination is by (b) _____

_____ .

22. Company P acquired all of the outstanding shares of the common stock (par $10) of Company S. At that date Company S reported 12,000 shares outstanding and retained earnings of $50,000. Company P common stock has a par value of $2 per share. Company S stock was selling for $16 per share. Complete the acquisition journal entry by Company P under two different assumptions:

Accounts	Combination Accomplished by—			
	Pooling of Interests (share for share exchange)		Purchase (paid cash for market price)	
Investment in Company S stock				
Common stock				
Cash				
Contributed capital from pooling				

23. Usually there is more depreciation expense on the consolidated income statement when the combination was a purchase than when it was a pooling of interests. _____ T; _____ F

24. Usually there is "goodwill amortization expense" on the consolidated income statement when the combination was a purchase rather than a pooling of interests. _____ T; _____ F

25. Company P purchased all of the common stock of Company S for $59,000 cash. At the date of purchase Company S had outstanding 5,000 shares of $6 par value common stock and retained earnings of $10,000. Company S had assets with a book value of $60,000 that had a market value of $64,000 and liabilities of $20,000 (assumed by Company P). Compute the amount of goodwill purchased.

26. On January 1, 19D, Company A acquired all of the common stock of Company B for $38,000 cash. The acquisition was recorded by Company A as follows:

Investment in Company B stock (3,000 shares)   38,000
      Cash   38,000

At date of acquisition the current market value of the equipment of Company B was $13,000 and the market value of the inventory was $14,000. Complete the following form to develop the consolidated balance sheet immediately after acquisition:

Combination by _____

| | Separate Statements | | | Consolidated Balance Sheet |
	Company A	Company B	Eliminations	
Assets:				
Cash	$ 10,000	$ 9,000		
Receivable from Co. B	4,000			
Inventory	40,000	16,000		
Investment in Co. B	38,000			
Equipment (net)	30,000	6,000		
Goodwill				
Total	$122,000	$31,000		
Liabilities:				
Accounts payable	$ 12,000	$ 2,000		
Payable to Co. A		4,000		
Stockholders' equity:				
Common stock:				
Co. A (par $10)	80,000			
Co. B (par $5)		15,000		
Retained earnings:				
Company A	30,000			
Company B		10,000		
Total	$122,000	$31,000		

27. Match each of the following accounting terms with its proper definition by inserting the letter which identifies the definition in the space next to the term.

Accounting Terms

_____ (1) Consolidation

_____ (2) Control

_____ (3) Goodwill

_____ (4) Minority interest

_____ (5) Parent company

_____ (6) Pooling of interests

_____ (7) Purchase

_____ (8) Subsidiary

Definitions

A. It is presumed to exist when more than 50 percent of the voting stock of an entity is owned by one investor

B. An acquisition that is completed by purchasing subsidiary company stock for cash

C. The company that has a significant investment in a subsidiary company

D. An acquisition that is completed by exchanging parent company stock for subsidiary voting capital stock

E. The accounting process of combining financial statements from related companies into a single set of financial statements

F. The company that is owned by a parent company as evidenced by 50 percent or more of the voting capital stock

G. The amount that was paid for the good reputation and customer appeal of an acquired company

H. The proportionate share of both the earnings and the contributed capital of the subsidiary that is not owned by the parent

Statement of Cash Flows

PURPOSE OF THIS CHAPTER

The previous chapters emphasized the income statement and the balance sheet. These statements are prepared directly from the balances contained in each ledger account. This chapter discusses the statement of cash flows (SCF) which is prepared by analyzing changes in various accounts.

HOW TO STUDY THIS CHAPTER

There are two reporting methods for the SCF: the direct method and the indirect method. There are two methods for preparing the SCF: the schedule approach and the spreadsheet. Because of these alternatives, many students find this topic to be confusing. As you read this chapter, be sure that you always know which reporting approach and which preparation approach you are studying.

STUDY OUTLINE OF THIS CHAPTER

Part A–Overview of the Statement of Cash Flows (SCF)

A. Purpose—to report cash inflows and outflows from the following activities:

1. Operating activities—cash flows directly related to earning income.
2. Investing activities—cash flows related to the acquisition of productive facilities used by the company and other noncash assets (exception—the acquisition of inventory is an operating activity).
3. Financing activities—cash flows related to the financing of the business by the owners and creditors (exception—the payment of interest expense is an operating activity).

B. Cash and cash equivalents are reported on the SCF. Cash equivalents are defined as short-term, highly liquid investments that are both:

1. Readily convertible to known accounts of cash.

2. So near their maturity that they present insignificant risk of changes in value because of changes in interest rates.

C. There are two methods for reporting cash flows from operating activities on the SCF.

1. Direct method which reports gross receipts (e.g., cash receipts from customers) and gross payments (e.g.., cash payments to suppliers). Exhibit 15–2 in the text shows an example of the direct method.

2. Indirect method which adjusts net income to compute net cash flow from operating activities. Exhibit 15–3 shows an example of the indirect method.

D. Preparation of the SCF, direct method—Schedule approach.

1. Revenue:

$$\text{Accrual Revenue} \begin{cases} + \text{ Decrease in receivable} \\ - \text{ Increase in receivable} \end{cases} = \text{ Cash revenue}$$

2. Expense:

$$\text{Accrual Expense} \begin{cases} + \text{ Decrease in payable} \\ - \text{ Increase in payable} \end{cases} = \text{ Cash expense}$$

3. Review Exhibit 15–5 for complete example.

E. Preparation of the SCF, direct method—Spreadsheet approach.

1. Prepared using the following steps:

   (a) Step 1 – set up four money columns as follows:

Beginning Balance 12/31/19A	Analysis of Change Debit	Credit	Ending Balance 12/31/19B

   (b) Step 2 – Copy income statement amounts in the middle two columns and the balance sheet amounts in the first and last columns.

   (c) Step 3 – Enter captions for the SCF below the income statement and balance sheet information.

   (d) Step 4 – Make debit-credit entries as illustrated in Exhibit 15–6.

2. Gains and losses must be associated with the activity that caused the gain or loss. For example, a gain on the sale of a truck is shown as an investing activity.

Part B–Preparation of the SCF, Indirect method

F. The indirect method starts with net income and reconciles net income with net cash flows from operating activities. Some examples are:

1. Add depreciation expense because it was subtracted from revenue to compute net income but it did not cause a cash outflow.

2. Subtract an increase in accounts receivable because it represents a portion of revenue that did not cause a cash inflow.

3.   Add an accounts payable increase because a portion of the related expense was not paid in cash.

G.   Preparation of the SCF under the schedule and spreadsheet approach. Review Exhibits 15–7 and 15–8.

H.   Certain exchanges do not have any cash flow effects. These transactions are called noncash investing and financing activities. They must be disclosed in narrative or schedule form.

15—Questions for Self Evaluation

These questions follow the sequence of the discussions in the chapter. However, they do not cover all of the points discussed in the chapter. After studying the chapter, try to answer each question to the best of your ability without referring again to the chapter. After answering all of them, turn to the solutions in the back and evaluate yourself. This should provide a valuable guide for deciding how much additional study you should commit to the chapter.

1. The SCF reports cash flows from the following activities:

   (a) _____

   (b) _____

   (c) _____

2. Cash flows from operating activities are directly related to

   _____

   _____

3. Cash received from customers is a cash flow from operating activities. _____ T _____ F

4. Dividends received in cash is a cash flow from investing activities. _____ T _____ F

5. Interest expense paid in cash is a cash flow from financing activities. _____ T _____ F

6. Dividends paid in cash is a cash flow from financing activities. _____ T _____ F

7. Cash paid for the purchase of inventory is a cash flow from investing activities.

   _____ T _____ F

8. Cash equivalents are defined as _____

   _____

   that meet two tests (a) _____

   _____ and (b) _____

   _____

9. The direct and indirect methods report different net amounts of cash from operating activities. _____ T _____ F

10. The _____ method reports gross cash payments and gross cash receipts in the cash flows from operating activities classification.

11. The _____ method adjusts net income to compute cash flows from operating activities.

12. The SCF is prepared directly from a trial balance. _____ T _____ F

13. Two approaches for preparing the SCF are (a) _____
_____ and (b) _____.

14. The purchase of a $100,000 building with a $100,000 mortgage is called a _____.
_____.

15. Gains and losses are reported on the SCF under _____
_____.

16. Complete the following formula:

Accrual revenue $\Big\langle$ (a) _____ receivable
(b) _____ receivable $\Big\rangle$ = Cash revenue

17. Complete the following formula:

Accrual expense $\Big\langle$ (a) _____ payable
(b) _____ payable $\Big\rangle$ Cash expense

18. Cost of goods sold for ABC Company was $12,000. During the year inventory increased $5,400 and accounts payable decreased $1,500. Cash payments to suppliers were $_____ .

For each of the following five questions, identify whether it is a plus or minus adjustment to net income to reconcile net income with cash flow from operating activities under the indirect method.

	when item increases	when item decreases
19. Accounts receivable	(a) _____	(b) _____
20. Accounts payable	(a) _____	(b) _____
21. Unearned revenue	(a) _____	(b) _____
22. Prepaid asset	(a) _____	(b) _____
23. Inventory	(a) _____	(b) _____

24. Noncash financing and investing activities are shown as both an inflow and outflow on the SCF. _____ T _____ F

25. Depreciation is added to net income under the direct method. _____ T _____ F

26. If there are no cash equivalents, the net change in cash reported on the SCF is the same as the change in the cash balance reported on the beginning and ending balance sheets.
_____ T _____ F

27. The accuracy of the SCF spreadsheet can be checked by adding the two analysis columns to verify that debits = credits. _____ T _____ F

28. The formal SCF can be prepared directly from the spreadsheet. _____ T _____ F

29. Match each of the following accounting terms with its proper definition by inserting the letter which identifies the definition in the space next to the term.

Accounting Terms

_____ (1) Cash equivalent

_____ (2) Cash flows from financing activities

_____ (3) Cash flows from investing activities

_____ (4) Cash flows from operating activities

_____ (5) Direct method

_____ (6) Indirect method

_____ (7) Noncash expense

_____ (8) Noncash investing and financing activities

_____ (9) Schedule approach

_____ (10) Spreadsheet approach

_____ (11) Statement of cash flows

Definitions

A. Inflows and outflows related to earning net income.

B. Used to develop the SCF; efficient method in simple cases.

C. Adjusts net income to compute cash flows from operating activities.

D. An expense that does not cause an immediate cash outflow; for example, depreciation expense.

E. Used to develop the SCF; widely used in practice.

F. Transactions that do not have direct cash flow effects; reported on the SCF in narrative or schedule form.

G. A short-term, highly liquid investment with original maturity of less than three months. SCF reports changes in cash and cash equivalents.

H. Inflows and outflows related to the acquisition or sale of productive facilities and making or collecting loans.

I. Reports components of cash flows from operating activities as gross receipts and gross payments.

J. A primary financial statement that reports cash inflows and outflows from operating, financing, and investing activities.

K. Inflows and outflows related to how cash was obtained to finance the enterprise.

16

Using and Interpreting Financial Statements

PURPOSE OF THIS CHAPTER

Throughout the preceding chapters, we emphasized the conceptual basis of accounting. An understanding of the rationale underlying accounting is important for both preparers and users of financial statements. In this chapter we introduce the use and analysis of financial statements. Many widely used analytical techniques are discussed and illustrated. As you study this chapter, you will see that an understanding of accounting rules and concepts is essential for effective analysis of financial statements.

HOW TO STUDY THIS CHAPTER

This chapter discusses the use and interpretation of financial statements. You should study it carefully in the light of the knowledge gained in the preceding 15 chapters because it is particularly relevant from the statement user's viewpoint. You should learn the common ratios given and how to interpret them.

STUDY OUTLINE OF THIS CHAPTER

A. The basic purpose of financial statements is to help the decision maker make better decisions. Users are interested in three types of information:

1. Information about past performance—past performance should be reported in detail.
2. Information about the present condition of the business—how the business stands today—what are the assets, debts, etc.?
3. Information about the future performance of the business—to help predict future potentials of the business to earn income, generate cash, and pay dividends.

B.   Statement users (decision makers) primarily are:

1.   Investors—including present and potential owners—usually invest to (a) receive income in the future (e.g. dividends), and (b) receive increases in the market value of their investment (e.g., share prices).

2.   Creditors—financial institutions and individuals that make short-term, and long-term loans to the enterprise to (a) receive interest revenue periodically and (b) receive the principal of the loan at maturity date.

3.   When making their decisions to invest, or to lend, the statement users primarily make a projection of the expected future net cash flows of the entity, because their expected returns are cash.

C.   When making decisions, investors should consider a variety of factors:

1.   Economy-wide factors—such as growth in the gross national product and the unemployment rate.

2.   Industry factors—some events have a major impact on each company within an industry, but only a minor impact on other companies.

3.   Individual company factors—may be either financial or nonfinancial.

D. Analysis of financial statements is a technique widely used by decision makers. The analysis provides an important basis for understanding the present condition of the business and projecting its future performance (e.g., cash flows). Analysis primarily involves two techniques:

1. Comparative statements—the presentation, at the end of each period, of the financial statements for the current year and one or more prior years. These tend to reveal trends in such factors as sales, expenses, net income, EPS, assets, debt, owners' equity, and sources and uses of funds (e.g., cash).

2. Ratio or percentage analysis.

E. The objective of ratio analysis is to reveal significant relationships between amounts selected from the financial statements.

1. A ratio, or percentage, is derived by dividing one amount (the numerator) by another amount (the denominator), which is known as the base amount. *Example:*

$$\frac{\text{Net income}}{\text{Net sales revenue}} = \frac{\$10,000}{\$100,000} = 10\%$$

This ratio is called the profit margin. It indicates that net income is 10 percent of sales revenue. Notice that net sales revenue is the base amount.

2. A ratio may be related to amounts from the same statement, as above (income statement), or it may relate to amounts from different statements. *Example*:

$$\frac{\text{Net income}}{\text{Owners' equity}} = \frac{\$10,000}{\$50,000} = 20\%$$

This ratio is called the return on owners' investment. One amount was taken from the income statement; the other from the balance sheet. Owners' equity is the base amount. It can be said that the company earned a 20 percent rate of return on the resources provided by the owners.

F. A large number of ratios, or percentages, can be computed from a single set of financial statements. However, only a few are widely used.

1. Component percentages—This involves the computation of a separate ratio for each line on a financial statement. For example, component percentages for an income statement are:

Sales revenue (the base amount)		$200,000 100%
Less expenses:		
Cost of goods sold	$140,000	70
Operating expenses	28,000	14
Financial expenses	4,000	2
Income tax expense	8,000	4
Total expenses		180,000 90
Net income		$ 20,000 10*

----

*Profit margin.

2. Some widely used ratios are:

Title	Computation
(a) Tests of profitability:	
(1) Return on owners' investment (ROI_0)	Income ÷ Average owners' equity
(2) Return on total investment (ROI_T)	[Income + Interest expense (net of income tax)] ÷ Average total assets
(3) Financial leverage ($ROI_0 - ROI_T$)	Return on owners' investment − Return on total investment
(4) Earnings per share (EPS)	Income ÷ Average shares of common stock outstanding
(5) Profit margin	Income ÷ Net sales revenue
(b) Tests of liquidity:	
(6) Current ratio	Current assets ÷ Current liabilities
(7) Quick (acid test) ratio	Quick assets ÷ Current liabilities
(8) Receivable turnover	Net credit sales ÷ Average net receivables
(9) Inventory turnover	Cost of goods sold ÷ Average inventory
(c) Tests of solvency and equity position:	
(10) Debt/equity ratio	Total liabilities ÷ Total owners' equity
(11) Owners' equity to total equity	Total owners' equity ÷ Total equities
(12) Creditors' equity to total equity	Total creditors' equity ÷ Total equities (i.e., total liabilities)

	Title	Computation

(d) **Market tests:**

(13) Price-earnings ratio (P/E ratio)   Current market price per share ÷ Earnings per share

(14) Dividend yield   Dividends per share ÷ Market price per share

(e) **Miscellaneous ratio:**

(15) Book value per common share   Owners' equity related to common stock ÷ Outstanding shares of common stock

3. The questions for self evaluation, which follow for this chapter, provide you with an illustration of the computation of each of the above 15 ratios.

4. The EPS ratio, return on investment ratios, debt/equity ratio, and P/E ratio, are considered to be especially important by many investors and creditors.

5. Ratios should be evaluated carefully against some standard. Users must decide whether the ratio for a particular company is reasonable, too high, or too low. The ratios of a company usually are compared with:

(a) Historical ratios of the company itself (ratios of prior years).
(b) Judgment—experience of the user.
(c) Planned or budgeted ratios developed for the company.
(d) External ratios for other companies and the industry average.

16—Questions for Self Evaluation

These questions follow the sequence of the discussions in the chapter. However, they do not cover all of the points discussed in the chapter. After studying the chapter, try to answer each question to the best of your ability without referring again to the chapter. After answering all of them, turn to the solutions in the back and evaluate yourself. This should provide a valuable guide for deciding how much additional study you should commit to the chapter.

1. Users of financial statements are interested in three types of information:

    (a) _____

    (b) _____

    (c) _____

2. Compute component percentages for the following statements:

Income Statement		Component Percentages	Balance Sheet (Partial)		Component Percentages
Sales revenue	$40,000	_____	Cash	$19,200	_____
Expenses:			Operational assets	68,800	_____
Cost of goods			Accumulated		
sold	(20,000)	_____	depreciation	(20,000)	_____
Remaining			Patent	8,000	_____
expenses	(16,000)	_____			
			Other assets	4,000	_____
Net income	$ 4,000	_____			
			Total assets	$80,000	_____

3. Compute the following items selected from comparative financial statements:

	Year		Increase (Decrease) 19B over 19A	
	19B	19A	Amount	Percent
Income statement:				
Sales revenue	$ 63,000	$ 60,000	_____	_____
Expenses	49,500	50,000	_____	_____
Net income	$ 13,500	$ 10,000	_____	_____
Balance sheet:				
Liabilities....................	$ 7,000	$ 10,000	_____	_____
Common stock	120,000	100,000	_____	_____
Retained earnings	30,000	40,000	_____	_____
Total.......................	$157,000	$150,000	_____	_____

4. The return on investment, profit margin, and EPS ratios are called the tests of _____ _____ .

5. The price-earnings and dividend yield ratios are called the _____ tests.

6. The current, quick, and turnover ratios are called the tests of _____ .

7. Return on investment ratios are regarded as the most important tests of profitability because they relate to both (a) _____ and (b) _____ .

8. The profit margin ratio is deficient as a test of profitability because it does not take into account the _____ _____ .

9. There are two primary tests of current liquidity. They are the (a) _____ ratio, and the (b) _____ ratio.

10. The _____ ratio is a measure of the effectiveness of the credit and collection activities.

11. A measure of the time merchandise remains on hand is called the _____ _____ .

12. The _____ ratio measures the balance attained by the management between resources provided by creditors versus owners.

13. A company with a high return on owners' investment when compared to return on total investment indicates positive _____ .

14. The two primary market ratios are identified to the left. Give their computation to the right.

    (a) The "Yield" _____

    (b) The "Multiple" _____

15. The higher a ratio is, the more favorable it is. _____ T; _____ F

16. Based upon the following data complete the table given below. Show computations and the ratio for each.

Income Statement

(a)	Sales revenue	$100,000
	Cost of goods sold	60,000
	Gross margin..........	40,000
(b)	Expenses	30,000
	Net income	$ 10,000

Explanatory Notes:
(a) Includes credit sales, $40,000
(b) Includes interest expense, $600
(c) The beginning accounts receivable balance was $14,000
(d) The beginning inventory was $11,000
(e) The market price per share was $65
(f) Dividends paid per share during the year, $2.60

Balance Sheet

Assets

	Cash	$ 5,000
(c)	Accounts receivable (net) ...	10,000
(d)	Inventory	15,000
	Plant equipment (net)	150,000
	Other assets	20,000
	Total	$200,000

Liabilities

	Accounts payable	$ 20,000
	Bonds payable.............	50,000

Stockholders' Equity

(e)	Common stock (par $100)...	100,000
(f)	Retained earnings	30,000
	Total	$200,000

16. (continued)

Use the above data to compute the following ratios (round to two places):

Item	Computations	Answer
Tests of profitability:		
(1) Return on owners' investment		
(2) Return on total investment		
(3) Financial leverage		
(4) Earnings per share		
(5) Profit margin		
Tests of liquidity:		
(6) Current ratio		
(7) Quick ratio		
(8) Receivable turnover		
(9) Inventory turnover		
Tests of solvency and equity position:		
(10) Debt/equity ratio		
(11) Owners' equity to total equity		
(12) Creditors' equity to total equity		
Market tests:		
(13) Price/earnings ratio		
(14) Dividend yield		
Miscellaneous ratio:		
(15) Book value per common share		

17. In respect to the evaluation and meaning of specific ratios, match the following:

Ratio	Meaning
(a) _____ Return on owners' investment	A. Indicator of future market performance (earnings capitalization) of the stock.
(b) _____ Profit margin	B. A measure of liquidity related to the current items on the balance sheet.
(c) _____ EPS	C. Effectiveness of credits and collections.
(d) _____ Financial leverage	D. A fundamental test of profitability because it includes both income and investment.
(e) _____ Current ratio	E. A measure of profitability expressed for a single share of common stock.
(f) _____ Receivable turnover	F. Measures common stockholders' equity for a single share of stock.
(g) _____ Debt/equity ratio	G. Profitability related to sales revenue, but does not consider resources used.
(h) _____ Book value per common share	H. The advantage (or disadvantage) for the stockholders which derives from borrowing at a lower rate than is earned on total resources employed.
(i) _____ Price/earnings ratio	I. The proportion of total resources provided by creditors, compared with owners.
(j) _____ Dividend yield ratio	J. The relationship between past dividends paid per year and the current market price of the shares.

18. Match each of the following accounting terms with its proper definition by inserting the letter which identifies the definition in the space next to the term.

Accounting Terms

_____ (1) Common ratios

_____ (2) Comparative statements

_____ (3) Component percentages

_____ (4) Long-term summaries

_____ (5) Market tests

_____ (6) Ratio analysis

_____ (7) Tests of liquidity

_____ (8) Tests of solvency

Definitions

A. Summaries of basic accounting data for many years (typically 10 years)

B. Ratios that measure a company's ability to meet its long-term obligations

C. Financial statements for several years, presented side by side for comparative purposes

D. Ratios that measure a company's ability to meet its currently maturing obligations

E. Selected ratios that are used widely

F. A percentage that expresses each item on a particular statement as a percent of a single base amount

G. Ratios that measure the "market worth" of a share of stock

H. An analytical tool designed to identify significant relationships between two financial statement amounts

Answers to Questions for Self Evaluation

Chapter 1

1. (b) record, (c) report

2. F, the primary purpose is to provide information to aid in decision making.

3. F, accounting records some events that are not transactions such as depreciation expense.

4. For accounting measurement purposes, the particular entity being accounted for is distinguished carefully from all similar and related entities and parties.

5. (1) B; (2) C; (3) A

6. T

7. T

8. (1) Certified Public Accountant
   (2) General Accounting Office (a regulatory agency)
   (3) American Institute of CPA's
   (4) Financial Accounting Standards Board
   (5) Securities and Exchange Commission
   (6) Certified Management Accountant
   (7) American Accounting Association
   (8) Generally Accepted Accounting Principles
   (9) Financial Executives Institute

9. (1) Income statement
   (2) Balance sheet
   (3) Statement of cash flows

10. F, ($100,000 − $60,000) × (1.00 − .30) = $28,000

11. D ($150,000 − $90,000) ÷ 20,000 shares = $3.00

12. ($90,000 − $60,000) ÷ $2.00 = 15,000 shares

13. $500,000 − $350,000 = $150,000

14. $18,000 ÷ 12 years = $1,500

15. ($30,000 − $24,000) ÷ $30,000 = 20%

16. $70,000 + $100,000 + $25,000 = $195,000

17. $40,000; Contributed capital in excess of par

18. (1) cash flows from operating activities, (2) cash flows from investing activities, (3) cash flows from financing activities

19. Balance sheet

20. Income statement

21. Statement of cash flows

22. (a) $60,000 − $51,000 = $9,000; (b) $9,000 ÷ 5,000 shares = $1.80

23.

Item	Revenue	Expense	Neither
(a)			✓
(b)	✓		
(c)		✓	
(d)		✓	
(e)	✓		
(f)			✓
(g)		✓	
(h)	✓		
(i)			✓
(j)		✓	
(k)	✓		
(l)		✓	
(m)	✓		

24. financial

25. $75,000 + $25,000 = \underline{$100,000}$

26. (a) assets;   (b) liabilities

27. $12,000 − $4,000 = \underline{$8,000}$

28. Account payable; note payable

29. Owners' equity

30. (a) contributed capital;   (b) retained earnings

31.

(1)	I	(7)	T	(13)	O	(20)	R
(2)	E	(8)	C	(14)	Z	(21)	Y
(3)	N	(9)	G	(15)	S	(22)	D
(4)	U	(10)	J	(16)	A	(23)	W
(5)	H	(11)	M	(17)	L	(24)	P
(6)	B	(12)	X	(18)	V	(25)	K
				(19)	AA	(26)	Q

Chapter 2

1. F, all exchange transactions have a dual economic effect.

2. source or supporting documents

3. Assets = Liabilities + Owners' Equity

4.

Transaction	Assets	=	Liabilities	+	Owners' Equity
(a)	$+5,000 (Cash)		$		$+5,000 (Capital stock)
(b)	+2,000 (Machine)		+2,000 (Accounts payable)		
(c)	+4,000 (Cash +3,000 Account receiv- able +1,000)				+4,000 (Service revenue)
(d)	−2,000 (Cash)		+ 500 (Account payable)		−2,500 (Expense)
(e)	+6,000 (Cash)		+6,000 (Note payable)		
(f)	− 400 (Machine)				− 400 (Expense)
Totals	$ 14,600		$8,500		$6,100

5. journalizing

DATE		ACCOUNT TITLES AND EXPLANATION	FO-LIO	DEBIT	CREDIT
Jan.	7	Cash		8 0 0 0	
		Service revenues			8 0 0 0
		Collected cash for service revenues.			
Jan.	12	Operational asset, truck		3 5 0 0	
		Cash			3 5 0 0
		Purchased a truck for business use.			
Jan.	15	Cash		4 0 0 0	
		Note payable			4 0 0 0
		Borrowed cash on 15% note.			
Jan.	28	Cash		5 0 0 0	
		Accounts receivable		1 0 0 0	
		Service revenue			6 0 0 0
		Services rendered; partial collection.			
Jan.	30	Expenses		1 1 0 0 0	
		Cash			1 1 0 0 0
		Paid expenses.			

7.

Cash				Notes Payable			Capital Stock, Nopar	
(a)	25,000	(d)	7,500		(b)	5,000	(a)	25,000
(b)	5,000							
(c)	11,000							

Accounts Receivable		Accounts Payable		Revenues	
(c)	1,000		(d) 500	(c)	12,000

Expenses	
(d)	8,000

8. credit; debit

9. (a) assets = liabilities + owners' equity
   (b) debits = credits

10. (a) owners' equity
    (b) assets
    (c) liabilities
    (d) owners' equity
    (e) liabilities; owners' equity

11. *Journal:*   *Folio*
    Jan. 10, 19A   101
                     302
    Jan. 12, 19A   404
                     101
    Jan. 15, 19A   101
                     105
    Jan. 19, 19A   203
                     101

    Ledger:

Cash		No. 101
5,000	3,000	
1,000	2,000	

Accounts Receivable	No. 105
	1,000

Accounts Payable		No. 203
	2,000	

Revenues	No. 302
	5,000

Expenses		No. 404
3,000		

12. | Item | Decreases | Increases |
    |---|---|---|
    | (a) | Debit | Credit |
    | (b) | Credit | Debit |
    | (c) | Debit | Credit |
    | (d) | Credit | Debit |
    | (e) | Debit | Credit |

13. T

14. F, increases expenses but decreases owners' equity.

15. (a) $9,000 \div 3$ years $= \underline{\$3,000}$

    (b) $15,000 \div \$3,000 = \underline{5}$ years

16. | (1) J | (4) I | (7) F | (10) F |
    |---|---|---|---|
    | (2) H | (5) C | (8) B | |
    | (3) G | (6) A | (9) D | |

Chapter 3

1. (a) C; (b) B; (c) A

2. journalizing; posting

3. original entry; final entry

4. F, transaction analysis must occur prior to journalizing.

5. (a) 3; (b) 6; (c) 2; (d) 4; (e) 5; (f) 1

6. (a) journal; (b) ledger

7. (a) Check on the equality of debits and credits in the ledger
   (b) Provide data in a convenient form to prepare the financial statements

8. F, it indicates that an error has been made.

9. assessing the future prospects of the enterprise

10. 7; 2; 1; 3; 4; 6; 5

11. The cost of merchandise that was sold during the period

12. (a) unusual in nature;   (b) infrequent in occurrence

13. (a) income tax effect on normal operations
    (b) income tax effect on extraordinary items

14. (a) cost of goods sold;   (b) $25,000

15. Earnings per share (EPS):

16. (a)($50,000 + $10,000) $\times$ 30% = $\underline{\$18,000}$
    (b) ($50,000 - $10,000) $\times$ 30% = $\underline{\$12,000}$

17. F, should be "For the Year Ended December 31, 19A".

18. F, the accounting year may end on any date.

19. T

20. F, should be "At December 31, 19XX".

21. T, they are reported only on the income statement.

22. Extraordinary items

23. (a) Long-term investments and funds
    (b) Tangible operational (i.e., fixed) assets
    (c) Intangible operational assets
    (d) Deferred charges
    (e) Other assets
    (f) Current liabilities
    (g) Long-term liabilities
    (h) Contributed capital
    (i) Retained earnings

24. liquidity

25. Retained earnings

26.
(1)	E	(5)	K	(9)	G	(13)	L
(2)	C	(6)	A	(10)	D		
(3)	B	(7)	H	(11)	M		
(4)	J	(8)	I	(12)	F		

Chapter 4

1. F, accumulated depreciation reflects cumulative depreciation to date.

2. matching

3. 19B, $\underline{$600}$ (1/2 year); 19C, $\underline{$1,200}$ (full year)

4.
Situation	19A	19B	19C
(a)	$3,000 (½ yr.)	$6,000 (1 yr.)	$ 6,000 (1 yr.)
(b)	3,000 (½ yr.)	9,000 (1 ½ yrs.)	15,000 (2 ½ yrs.)
(c)	1,200 (½ yr.)	2,400 (1 yr.)	1,200 (½ yr.)
(d)	3,600 (1 ½ yrs.)	1,200 (½ yr.)	-0-
(e)	-0-	1,600 (4 mos.)	800 (2 mos.)
(f)	-0-	800 (2 mos.)	-0-
(g)	600 (½ yr.)	1,200 (1 yr.)	600 (½ yr.)
(h)	600 (½ yr.)	600 (½ yr.)	-0-

5.
Property tax expense (expense)	2,400	
Property tax payable (liability)		2,400

   $4,800 × 6/12 = $2,400.

6. (a) December 31, 19A

Insurance expense ($1,200 × 6/24 = $300)	300	
Prepaid insurance		300

   (b) (1) Apportioned a part of prepaid insurance to expense for matching purposes.
   (2) Adjusted the asset account, Prepaid insurance, to the correct amount still prepaid at the end of 19A (i.e., $1,200 − $300 = $900).

7. (a) December 31, 19A

Interest expense ($10,000 × 12% × 3/12)	300	
Interest payable		300

8.
	Verification	Debit	Credit
(1)	$400 × 12/24 = $200	i	a
(2)	$4,000 ÷ 5 years = $800	b	d
(3)	$20 + $400 − $100 = $320	c	h
(4)	$700 as given	j	e
(5)	$2,000 × 12% × 6/12 = $120	l	f
(6)	$2,400 × 1/3 = $800	m	g
(7)	$400 × 2 = $800	n	g

9. (a) December 31, 19B:

Depreciation expense ($10,000 − $400) ÷ 8 years	1,200	
Accumulated depreciation		1,200

   (b) (1) Apportions a part of the cost of the equipment to 19B expense.

   (2) Records the reduction of the cost of the asset, equipment, for its use for the year. The amount is entered in a *contra* account rather than directly in the equipment account.

   (c) Balance, accumulated depreciation, ($10,000 − $400) × 2/8 = $2,400. It is a contra asset account because it is deducted from (an offset to) the related asset account, equipment.

   (d) Book value; 19A, $10,000 − $1,200 = $8,800; 19B, $10,000 − ($1,200 + $1,200) = $7,600.

10. Interest receivable 50
         Interest revenue ($1,000 × 15% × 4/12 50

11. (a) December 31, 19A
          Wage expense 850
          Wages payable 850

     (b) (1) Records this additional amount to expense for matching with 19A revenues.
          (2) Records the liability for unpaid wages at the end of 19A (payment will be made on the next payroll date).

12. (a) income statement; (b) statement of cash flows

13. time-period

14. interim

15. adjusting entries

16. F, the revenue principle takes precedence.

17. F, service revenue should be recognized as performed; therefore, only part of the revenue should be included in 19X revenues.

18. F, there is no reason why the two should coincide.

19. T

20. T

21. (a) Separate entity assumption
     (b) Continuity assumption
     (c) Unit-of-measure assumption
     (d) Time period assumption

22. (a) Cost principle
     (b) Revenue principle
     (c) Matching principle
     (d) Full-disclosure principle

23. Cost-benefit

24. Relevance

25. Reliability

26. (1) J   (8) U   (15) R
     (2) B   (9) P   (16) G
     (3) S   (10) O   (17) Q
     (4) F   (11) K   (18) E
     (5) T   (12) C   (19) N
     (6) A   (13) I   (20) H
     (7) M   (14) D   (21) L

Chapter 5

1. hardware; software

2. (a) 9; (b) 7; (c) 3; (d) 6; (e) 4; (f) 10; (g) 1; (h) 8; (i) 5; (j) 2

3. F, it is optional.

4. T

5. unadjusted trial balance (or ledger accounts)

6. F, completed at the end of the period.

7. (a) Income statement
   (b) Statement of retained earnings
   (c) Balance sheet

8. journal; ledger

9. (a)

NEST CORPORATION
Statement of Retained Earnings
For the Year Ended December 31, 19A

Balance retained earnings, January 1, 19A	$20,000
Add: Net income for 19A	15,000
Total..	35,000
Less: Dividends declared and paid during 19A	12,000
Balance retained earnings, December 31, 19A	$23,000

(b) December 31, 19A, balance, $23,000.

(c) (1) To close Income summary:

Income summary	15,000	
Retained earnings..........................		15,000

   (2) To close Dividends paid:

Retained earnings..........................	12,000	
Dividends paid		12,000

10. real or permanent; temporary or nominal

11. income statement (i.e., temporary or nominal); balance sheet (i.e., permanent or real)

12. F, extended to one or the other.

13. F, only the nominal accounts are closed.

14. (a) revenue accounts
    (b) income summary

15.

Journal

December 31, 19B:
    To close revenues:
       (n) Revenues
             (o) Income summary
	30,000	30,000

To close expenses:
       (o) Income summary
             (f) Expenses
	20,000	20,000

To close income summary:
       (o) Income summary
           (m) Retained earnings
	10,000	10,000

To close dividends paid:
       (m) Retained earnings
          (g) Dividends paid
	5,000	5,000

16.

(1) D	(5) F	(9) E
(2) J	(6) C	(10) K
(3) A	(7) L	(11) B
(4) H	(8) I	(12) G

Chapter 6

1. (a) sale transaction occurs (ownership transferred)
   (b) cash equivalent price (received or to be received)

2. F, service revenue is recognized as the services are performed.

3. Gross margin on sales

4. Net sales revenue

5. ($80,000 − $3,000) − $30,000 = $47,000

6. $50,000 − ($50,000 × 0.60) = $20,000

7. Three percent discount on the invoice (sale) price if paid within 10 days and, if not paid in this period, the full amount is payable in 30 days (from date of sale).

8. (a)
Cash...	12,000	
Accounts receivable	4,000	
Sales revenue		16,000

   (b)
Cash...	4,000	
Accounts receivable		4,000

9. (a)
Accounts receivable ($400 × 0.98)	392	
Sales revenue		392

   (b)
Cash...	392	
Accounts receivable		392

   (c)
Cash...	400	
Accounts receivable		392
Interest revenue (or Sales discount revenue)		8

10. F, sales revenue does not include financing charges.

11. F, cash discounts relate to credit sales, whereas trade discounts relate to sales price determinations.

12. The sales revenue recognized for the period (for credit sales) may not be fully realized (i.e., collected) because one or more customers do not pay their bill in full. This bad debt expense must be matched with the revenue of the period which caused it. Because the amount of uncollectible receivables cannot be known until a later period, the amount of bad debt expense must be estimated and recorded at the end of the current period.

13. Allowance for doubtful accounts.

14. E, $15,000 + $30,000 + $35,000 + $1,200 − $1,500 = $79,700

15. (a) yes
    (b) matching principle

16. (a)
Bad debt expense ($20,000 × 1¼%)	250	
Allowance for doubtful accounts....................		250

   (b)
Allowance for doubtful accounts....................	100	
Accounts receivable (J. Doe)		100

The bad debt expense was recorded at the end of 19D on the basis of an estimate (total estimate for all 19D bad debts was $250).

17. (a) $9,100
    (b) $600
    (c) $8,500; $8,500
    (d) $350

18. F, the expense account balance is for the current year only; the allowance account is a cumulative balance.

19. T

20. Beginning inventory (given) $20,000
    (a) Purchases ($80,000 − $20,000)....................... 60,000
         Goods available for sale (given).................... 80,000
         Ending inventory ($20,000 × 70%) 14,000
    (b) Cost of goods sold ($80,000 − $14,000).............. $66,000

21. periodic inventory system; perpetual inventory system

22. T

23. F, the "purchases" account is used under the periodic system only.

24. T

25. T

26. Beginning inventory (BI) + Purchases (P) − Ending inventory (EI) = Cost of goods sold (CGS)

27. (a) Purchases, $4,000 + ($1,000 × 0.97) 4,970
         Cash...   4,000
         Accounts payable ($1,000 × 0.97).................   970

    (b) Accounts payable 970
         Cash...   970

    (c) Accounts payable 970
         Interest expense (or Purchase discount lost) 30
         Cash...   1,000

28.

Accounts	(a) Periodic Debit	(a) Periodic Credit	(b) Perpetual Debit	(b) Perpetual Credit
(1) Purchases	30,000			
Merchandise inventory			30,000	
Cash..		30,000		30,000
(2) Cash..	35,000		35,000	
Sales revenue		35,000		35,000
Cost of goods sold	Not applicable—accounted for at end of period when physical inventory is taken.		15,000	
Merchandise inventory (½ × $30,000)				15,000
(3) Cash ($30,000 × 1/20)..............................	1,500		1,500	
Purchase returns*		1,500		
Merchandise inventory				1,500
(4) Sales returns and allowances.........................	700		700	
Cash ($35,000 × 2%).................................		700		700
Merchandise inventory ($15,000 × 2%)	Not applicable—accounted for at end of period when physical inventory is taken.		300	
Cost of goods sold				300

*Contra account to purchases.

29. F, the inventory account changes during the period under the perpetual system but not the periodic system.

30. ending; beginning

31.

	Debit	Credit
Inventory shrinkage (or loss due to theft)	36	
Merchandise inventory (3 × $12)		36

32. (a) Periodic inventory system

Adjusting entries:

	Debit	Credit
Income summary	10,000	
Merchandise inventory (beginning)		10,000
Merchandise inventory	15,000	
Income summary		15,000

Closing entry:

	Debit	Credit
Income summary	70,000	
Purchases		70,000

(b) Perpetual inventory system:

Adjusting entries—none for these accounts.
Closing entry:

	Debit	Credit
Income summary	65,000	
Cost of goods sold		65,000

33.
(1)	N	(5)	E	(9)	H	(13)	J	(17)	F
(2)	L	(6)	B	(10)	Q	(14)	M		
(3)	G	(7)	K	(11)	C	(15)	A		
(4)	P	(8)	D	(12)	O	(16)	I		

Chapter 7

1. (1) D; (2) C; (3) B; (4) A

2. Include all, but only, goods to which the company has legal title regardless of location.

3. seller; buyer

4. consignor

5. A

6. Cost

7. ($50 × .98) + $4 = $53

8. (1) A: (2) B

9. detailed inventory records; a physical inventory count

10. B

11. specific identification method

12. oldest; newest

13. oldest; newest

14. purchase of the item

15. when costs are rising, LIFO provides a lower pretax income, hence a lower income tax payment (cash).

16. (1) B; (2) A

17. Goods available, 400 units − Sales, 300 units = 100 units in ending inventory.

    (b) $2,400 ÷ 400 units = $6 weighted average unit cost
          CGS = 300 × $6 = $1,800; EI = 100 × $6 = $600

    (c) CGS = (100 × $5) + (200 × $6) = $1,700
          EI = 100 × $7 = $700

    (d) CGS = (100 × $7) + (200 × $6) = $1,900
          EI = 100 × $5 = $500

18.

	Amount	Order of Computation
(a) Ending inventory ($70,000 − $58,000)...................	$12,000	3
(b) Cost of goods sold ($100,000 − $42,000)...............	58,000	2
(c) Gross margin on sales ($100,000 × 42%)	42,000	1

19.

	Perpetual	Periodic
(a)		√
(b)	√	
(c)	√	√
(d)	√	√
(e)		√
(f)	√	

20. F, $300 − $50 − $30 = $220

Inventory of used appliances	220	
Allowance for doubtful accounts		
(or loss on repossessions)......................................	25	
Accounts receivable		245

21. net realizable value (i.e., estimated sales price minus all costs to renovate and resell)

22. $80; lower of cost or market (LCM)

23. comparability

24. (a)

Store supplies inventory	900	
Cash..		900

    (b)

Store supplies expense ($400 + $900 − $325)	975	
Store supplies inventory		975

25. T

26. F, 19B income will be understated and 19C income will be overstated.

27. T

28. 19A: $8,000 − $1,100 = $6,900

    19B: $6,000 + $1,100 = $7,100

29. C, 19A: $20,000 + $5,000 = $25,000

      19B: $30,000 − $5,000 + $1,000 = $26,000

30.
(1)	D	(5)	H	(9)	M	(13)	E
(2)	N	(6)	F	(10)	I	(14)	J
(3)	P	(7)	O	(11)	G	(15)	L
(4)	B	(8)	K	(12)	C	(16)	A

Chapter 8

1. liquid

2.
(a)	Include	(g)	Include
(b)	Exclude	(h)	Exclude
(c)	Include	(i)	Exclude
(d)	Exclude	(j)	Include
(e)	Include	(k)	Include
(f)	Exclude	(l)	Include

3. next accounting period (year); normal operating cycle of the business

4. Internal control

5. (a) attain effective internal control of cash and (b) to minimize opportunities for theft

6. (a) deposit intact
   (b) make all cash payments

7. (a) a listing of all deposits made during the period
   (b) a listing of all checks cashed by the bank during the period
   (c) a running balance of the depositor's account
   (d) copies of all deposit slips and checks cashed
   (e) Given

8. petty cash fund

9. A compensating balance is when a bank, usually in making a loan, requires the depositor to maintain a minimum balance in the bank account during the period of the loan.

10. F, the reconciliation is made for ending balances.

11. T

12. (a)

Depositor's Books		Bank Statement	
Balance	$5,500	Balance	$7,309
Additions:		Additions:	
Note collected:		Deposits in transit ($20,000 − $18,000)	2,000
Principal	300		
Interest	24		
Deductions:		Deductions:	
Bank service charge	(15)	Outstanding checks ($19,500 − $16,000)	(3,500)
Correct cash balance	$5,809	Correct cash balance	$5,809

  (b) (1)   Cash 324

             Notes receivable............................. 300

             Interest revenue 24

      (2)   Expense—bank service charges.................. 15

             Cash 15

13. (a) marketability; (b) a planned short-term holding period

14. current assets; investments and funds

15. Current assets:
    Short-term investments, at cost (market value $2,300) $2,000

16. exception—conservatism

17. (a) Short-term investments 5,200
         Cash.   5,200

    (b) Cash ($1.50 × 500 shares).   750
         Investment revenue   750

    (c) Cash. 2,500
         Loss on sale of investments   100
         Short-term investments ($5,200 ÷ 2)   2,600

18. (a) Short-term investments 6,400
         Cash ($6,000 + $400).   6,400

    (b) Cash (800 shares × $1)   800
         Investment revenue   800

    (c) Unrealized loss on short-term investments.   400
         Allowance to reduce short-term investments to
           market.   400
         800 shares × ($8.00 − $7.50) = $400

19. negotiable

20. (a) maker;   (b) payee

21. (a) interest bearing
    (b) noninterest bearing

22. F, in business transactions, all notes require the payment of interest.

23. compensating balance

24. (a) Note receivable. 600.00
         Sales revenue 600.00

    (b) Interest receivable 22.50
         Interest revenue ($600 × 15% × 3/12) 22.50

    (c) Cash. 690.00
         Interest receivable (per b) 22.50
         Interest revenue ($600 × 15% × 9/12) 67.50
         Note receivable. 600.00

25. Cash 2,035
    Note receivable (trade)   2,000
    Interest revenue ($150 − $115 = $35)   35

    Computations:
    Principal amount $2,000
    Interest due at maturity ($2,000 × 15% × 6/12)   150
      Maturity value   2,150
    Discount ($2,150 × 16% × 4/12 = $115 rounded).   115
    Cash proceeds $2,035

26.
(1)	W	(6)	R	(11)	K	(16)	M	(21)	O
(2)	Q	(7)	A	(12)	T	(17)	D	(22)	P
(3)	F	(8)	E	(13)	G	(18)	J		
(4)	L	(9)	H	(14)	B	(19)	U		
(5)	N	(10)	V	(15)	I	(20)	S		

Chapter 9

1. T

2. (a) cost; (b) matching

3. operational assets

4. (a) asset; (b) depreciation expense

5. cash equivalent cost

6. Machine 128,000
        Cash ($50,000 + $3,000) 53,000
        Capital stock (5,000 shares × $15) 75,000

7. (a) $12,000 × 1/3 = $4,000; (b) $6,500

8. Tract A—$33,000 × ($13,000/$20,000) = $21,450
    Tract B—$33,000 × ($ 7,000/$20,000) = $11,550
        Total $33,000

9. F, intangible assets do not have a physical substance.

10. T

11. matching

12. (a) C; (b) A; (c) B; (d) D

13. (a) Tangible Operational Assets (or Property, Plant and Equipment):
         Machine $8,000
         Less: Accumulated depreciation ($8,000 × .90) × 3/5 = $4,320....   4,320 $3,680

    (b) Depreciation expense ($8,000 × .90) ÷ 5 years = $1,440

14. matching

15. (a) acquisition cost
    (b) residual value
    (c) useful life or expected output

16. (a) extraordinary
    (b) ordinary

17. Repair expense 400
    Machinery (or Accumulated depreciation) 3,500
       Cash...   3,900

18. Cash.. 1,900
    Accumulated depreciation ($4,800 × 4/6) 3,200
       Machinery   4,800
       Gain on disposal of operational asset   300

19. Case A:

Asset Y ($10,000 − $3,000) + $1,500	8,500	
Accumulated depreciation (Asset X).............................	3,000	
Asset X		10,000
Cash..		1,500

Case B:

Asset Y ($7,300 + $1,500)	8,800	
Accumulated depreciation (Asset X).............................	3,000	
Asset X		10,000
Cash..		1,500
Gain on disposal of operational asset		300

20. (a) $6,000,000 ÷ 10 million units = $0.60 per unit

    (b) 800,000 units × $0.60 = $480,000

    (c)

Depletion expense	480,000	
Mineral deposit (or Accumulated depletion)		480,000

21.

Patent amortization expense [$16,800 ÷ (15 − 3 yrs.)]	1,400	
Patent (or Accumulated amortization)		1,400

22. (a) C; (b) B; (c) D; (d) A; (e) G; (f) H; (g) F; (h) E

23. (a) cost; (b) shorter of the remaining legal or useful life

24. (a) natural resource; (b) depletion expense

25.

Depreciation expense..	2,620	
Accumulated depreciation, building		2,620

[$80,000 − ($2,400 − $1,000)] ÷ 30 years = $2,620

26. (a) Straight-line: ($1,200 − $300) ÷ 4 yrs. = $225

    (b) Productive output: $900 ÷ 1,000 units = $0.90; $0.90 × 300 units = $270

    (c) SYD $900 × 4/10 = $360

    (d) 200% DB 4 yrs. = 200% × 25% = 50%; $1,200 × 50% = $600

27. (a) An expenditure that will contribute to earning revenue for more than one accounting period. An asset account is debited.

    (b) An expenditure that will contribute to earning revenue for the current period only. An expense account is debited.

28.

(1)	K	(7)	G	(13)	F	(19)	Z	(25)	M
(2)	Y	(8)	O	(14)	X	(20)	N	(26)	W
(3)	U	(9)	R	(15)	I	(21)	Q	(27)	P
(4)	AA	(10)	E	(16)	A	(22)	H		
(5)	D	(11)	B	(17)	T	(23)	C		
(6)	J	(12)	V	(18)	L	(24)	S		

Chapter 10

1. economic benefits, assets, past transactions or events

2. (a) current liabilities;   (b) long-term liabilities

3. cost

4. F, the amount may be estimated rather than known.

5. one year of the balance sheet date; the normal operating cycle of the business; the longer

6. expense; paid or recorded

7. T

8. (a) $60,000 - $20,000 = $40,000

   (b) $60,000 ÷ $20,000 = 3 (to 1)

9. F, longer of one year or the normal operating cycle.

10. (a) December 31, 19A:

Wage expense	780	
Wages payable		780

   (b) January 10, 19B:

Wages payable*	780	
Wage expense	11,120	
Cash		11,900

   *Assuming no reversing entry was made on January 1, 19B

11. June 30, 19A:

Wage and salary expense	20,000	
Liability for income tax withheld		2,500
Liability for union dues withheld		400
FICA taxes payable—Employees		1,200
Cash		15,900

12. deferred or unearned revenue

13.

Rent revenue	1,750	
Rent revenue collected in advance (or Unearned rent revenue)		1,750

14. pledged certain assets

15. (a) February 1, 19A:

Cash	1,000	
Note payable		1,000

   (b) July 31, 19A:

Note payable	1,000	
Interest expense ($1,000 × 10% × 6/12)	50	
Cash		1,050

16. (a) Cash... 3,000
           Note payable   3,000

     (b) Interest expense ($3,000 × 12% × 5/12) 150
           Interest payable...............................   150

     (c) Note payable 3,000
           Interest payable (per above)* 150
           Interest expense ($3,000 × 12% × 7/12) 210
           Cash [$3,000 + ($3,000 × 12%)]   3,360

           *Assumes no reversing entry was made on January 1, 19B.

17. A debit, $600, because income tax expense for 19A was less than income tax payable

18. T, these are not timing differences; rather they are permanent differences.

19. F, the account may have a debit or a credit balance.

20. T

21. T

22. 19A:
       Income tax expense ($20,000 × 30%) 6,000
       Deferred income tax 1,500
           Income tax payable ($20,000 + $5,000) × 30%   7,500

     19B:
       Income tax expense ($35,000 × 30%) 10,500
           Deferred income tax   1,500
           Income tax payable ($35,000 − $5,000) × 30%   9,000

23. already occurred; occurrence of one or more future events or transactions.

24. T

25. interest; $2,000 × 8% = $160

26. (a), D; (b), A; (c), B; (d), C;

27. (a) $1,500 × 1.5869 (Table 10-1) = $2,380.35

     (b) $1,500 × 7.3359 (Table 10-3) = $11,003.85

     (c) $50,000 × 0.4972 (Table 10-2) = $24,860

     (d) $2,000 × 3.3121 (Table 10-4) = $6,624.20

28. (a) $100,000 × 1.9672 (use Table 10-1) = $196,720

     (b) Building fund....................................... 100,000
           Cash...   100,000

     (c) Building fund....................................... 7,000
           Interest revenue ($100,000 × 7%)...................   7,000

     (d) Building fund....................................... 7,490
           Interest revenue ($100,000 + $7,000) × 7%..........   7,490

     (e) $100,000 + $7,000 + $7,490 = $114,490

29. T, must be more than the sum of the 10 deposits.

30. (a) $30,000 \div P_{n=4} \atop i=10\%$ (3.1699) = $\underline{\$9,464}$ (Table 10-4)

(b) ($9,464 \times 4) - \$30,000 = \underline{\$7,856}$

31.

(1)	C	(5)	Q	(9)	P	(13)	L	(17)	E
(2)	H	(6)	A	(10)	F	(14)	J	(18)	M
(3)	K	(7)	I	(11)	G	(15)	B		
(4)	N	(8)	D	(12)	O	(16)	R		

Chapter 11

1. (a) underwriter; (b) trustee
2. T
3. serial
4. (a) callable; (b) redeemable
5. convertible
6. financial leverage
7. (a) current cash equivalent; (b) cost
8. (a) par; (b) premium; (c) discount
9. $8.5\% \times (1.00 - .30) = 5.95\%$

10.

	Stocks	Bonds
(a)	√	
(b)	√	
(c)		√
(d)		√
(e)		√
(f)	√	
(g)	√	
(h)		√
(i)	√	

11.

	Sold at 100	Sold at 97	Sold at 102
Cash	1,000	970	1,020
Discount on bonds		30	
Premium on bonds...........................			20
Bonds payable	1,000	1,000	1,000

12. par value
13. lower
14. T
15. matching

16. F, it decreases the effective interest rate to an amount which is less than the stated rate of interest.

17. F, the amount of discount amortized is added to the amount of cash paid to determine interest expense.

18.

Accounts	Sold at 100		Sold at 104		Sold at 97	
Interest expense	900		820		960	
Bond premium			80[a]			
Bond discount						60[b]
Cash		900		900		900

(a) $400 ÷ 5 yrs. = $80   (b) $300 ÷ 5 yrs. = $60

19. (a) Cash....................................... 1,000
      Bonds payable...................................   1,000

(b) Bond interest expense 30
      Cash ($1,000 × 3%)...............................   30
      (Entry repeated *each* June 30 and December 31)

(c) Cash....................................... 940
     Discount on bonds payable........................ 60
      Bonds payable...................................   1,000

(d) Bond interest expense 33
     Discount on bonds payable ($60 × 1/20)   3
     Cash ($1,000 × 3%)...............................   30
      (Entry repeated each June 30 and December 31)

(e) Cash....................................... 1,060
     Premium on bonds payable   60
     Bonds payable...................................   1,000

(f) Interest expense................................... 27
     Premium on bonds payable ($60 × 1/20) 3
     Cash ($1,000 × 3%)...............................   30
      (Entry repeated each June 30 and December 31)

20. (a) Twelve percent, as stated on the bond; this rate determines the cash interest to be paid annually (i.e., $1,000 × 12% = $120).

(b) Computation of the approximate effective or real rate of interest:
    Cash received at issuance .... $ 950
    Cash paid back:
      Principal at maturity $1,000
      Interest ($1,000 × 12% × 10 years) 1,200 2,200
    Difference—Amount of interest paid $1,250

    Effective or real interest: $1,250 ÷ 10 years = $125
                $125 ÷ $950 = 13.16% per year

21. Balance sheet:

    (a) Long-term liabilities:
         Bonds payable.. $40,000
         Add: Unamortized premium.............................. <u>2,800</u> $42,800

    (b) Long-term liabilities:
         Bonds payable.. $40,000
         Less: Unamortized discount .... <u>2,800</u> $37,200

22. T

23. T

24. (a) Cash [$100,000 + ($100,000 $\times$ 12% $\times$ 2/12 = $2,000)]   102,000
         Bonds payable (par)..............................   100,000
         Interest expense ($100,000 $\times$ 12% $\times$ 2/12)   2,000

    (b) Interest expense.................................... 6,000
         Cash ($100,000 $\times$ 12% $\times$ 6/12)   6,000

25. (a) ($100,000 $\times$ 12% $\times$ 6/12) $\times$ 2 = $12,000

    (b) 10 months

    (c) $100,000 $\times$ 12% $\times$ 10/12 = $10,000

    (d) The difference, $12,000 − $10,000 = $2,000 represents two months interest ($100,000 $\times$12% $\times$ 2/12) which is for the period between the date of the bonds and the issuance date. This is the amount of accrued interest prior to issuance date. The investor was entitled to only 10 months interest. The issuer was legally required to disburse $12,000 cash; however, the $2,000 accrued interest was collected at issuance date, which leaves interest expense of $12,000 − $2,000 = $10,000.

26. The buyer is entitled to interest for only the time the buyer holds the bond; however, the buyer will collect interest (cash) for a full interest period on the interest date following the date of purchase.

27. (a) October 1, 19A—Sale and issuance of bond:
         Cash ($10,000 $\times$ .98) 9,800
         Discount on bond payable   200
         Bond payable (par)   10,000

    (b) December 31, 19A—End of annual accounting period:
         Interest expense ($225 + $10) 235
         Discount on bond payable ($200 ÷ 5) $\times$ 3/12.....   10
         Accrued interest expense ($10,000 $\times$ 9% $\times$ 3/12)   225

28. E ($3,000 $\times$ 1.03) + ($3,000 $\times$ 8% $\times$ 2/12) = $3,090 + $40 = <u>$3,130</u>

29. B ($3,000 $\times$ 8% $\times$ 8/12 = $160) − [($90 ÷ 58 mos.) $\times$ 8 mos. = $12] = <u>$148</u>

30. bond sinking fund

31. (a) $300,000 ÷ 10.2598 = \underline{\$29,240}$

(b) Bond sinking fund.................................. 29,240.00
     Cash...   29,240.00

(c) Bond sinking fund.................................. 2,046.80
     Interest revenue ($29,240 × 7%)...................   2,046.80

32. investments and funds

33.

Date	Cash Interest Paid	Interest Expense	Effective-Interest Amortization	Net Liability
1/1/19A				$ 9,662
12/31/19A	$1,000	$1,159	$159	9,821
12/31/19B	1,000	1,179	179	10,000

34.

(1) H	(5) B	(9) A	(13) G	(17) J
(2) D	(6) I	(10) M	(14) C	(18) F
(3) K	(7) L	(11) C	(15) O	
(4) N	(8) P	(12) Q	(16) E	

Chapter 12

1. F, only a corporation must obtain a charter.

2. board of directors

3. F, the number of treasury shares equals the number of shares issued minus the number outstanding.

4. T

5. (a) common; (b) preferred

6. T, state laws forbid a discount upon original issue

7. (a) D   (d) F
   (b) A   (e) E
   (c) B   (f) C

8. F, some features are unfavorable, such as the lack of voting rights.

9. (a) Dividend preferences
   (b) Conversion privileges
   (c) Asset preferences
   (d) nonvoting specifications

10. convertible

11. F, there are differences in accounting for owners' equity for corporations, partnerships, and proprietorships.

12. (a) total amount invested by stockholders by the purchase of shares from the corporation
    (b) cumulative amount of net income less cumulative losses and less cumulative dividends

13. (a) contributed capital
    (b) preferred
    (c) 1,000 shares $\times$ \$10 = $\underline{\$10,000}$
    (d) authorized
    (e) preferred stock
    (f) \$10,000 + \$140,000 + \$6,000 = $\underline{\$156,000}$
    (g) earnings
    (h) \$156,000 + \$30,000 = $\underline{\$186,000}$

14. (a) No journal entries required; make separate memo notation for preferred and common stock.

    (b) Preferred stock:

Cash (500 shares $\times$ \$16)	8,000	
Preferred stock, par \$10 (500 shares $\times$ \$10)		5,000
Contributed capital in excess of par, preferred		
[500 shares $\times$ (\$16 − \$10)]		3,000

    Common stock:

Cash (10,000 shares $\times$ \$22).......................	220,000	
Common stock, nopar (10,000 shares)		220,000

15. negative (or contra) stockholders' equity

16. cash; stockholders' equity

17. (a) Treasury stock, common (100 shares × $18) 1,800
       Cash.. 1,800

    (b) Cash (50 shares × $25) 1,250
       Treasury stock, common (50 shares × $18) 900
       Contributed capital, treasury stock transactions
       [50 shares × ($25 − $18)] 350

    (c) (1) 50
       (2) treasury stock
       (3) 4,000 shares × $10 = $40,000
       (4) 4,000 shares × ($12 − $10) = $8,000
       (5) $40,000 + $8,000 = $48,000
       (6) Cost of treasury shares held (50 × $18) = $900
       (7) $48,000 + $25,000 − $900 = $72,100

18.   *Stockholders' Equity*

Contributed capital:
  Common stock, par $10, authorized 10,000 shares, issued 7,000
    shares, of which 100 shares are held as treasury stock $70,000
  Contributed capital in excess of par............................... 21,000
    Total contributed capital 91,000
Retained earnings 25,000
  Total... 116,000
Less cost of treasury stock held (100 shares) 1,700
  Total stockholders' equity $114,300

19. (a) Cash inflows from dividends on the shares
    (b) Cash inflows upon disposal (sale) of the shares

20. (a) Cash to pay the dividend
    (b) Retained earnings to cover the dividend

21. cash; retained earnings

22. cash; stockholders' equity

23. noncumulative

24. (a) B; (b) C

25.

Case	Preferred	Common	Total
A. Preference: $50,000 × 5% .... None left for common	$ 2,500	$ 0	$ 2,500
B. Preference... Balance to common ($6,000 − $2,500)	2,500 2,500	 3,500 3,500	2,500 3,500 6,000
C. In arrears—2 years .... Current year....................................... Balance to common .... Totals...	5,000 2,500 7,500	 7,400 7,400	5,000 2,500 7,400 14,900

26. increases; decreases

27. capitalizing

28. Retained earnings (1,000 shares × $35)   35,000

      Common stock (10,000 shares × 10% = 1,000 shares × $20) ...   20,000

      Contributed capital in excess of par   15,000

29. (a) $30;   40,000 shares [i.e., (10,000 × 3) + 10,000]

     (b) $30 ÷ 3 = $10;   30,000 shares

30.

Item	Increase	Decrease	No Effect
(a)			X
(b)			X
(c)			X
(d)			X
(e)			X
(f)	X		
(g)		X	

31. (a) declaration

     (b) payment

     (c) record

32. (a) stockholders' subsidiary record

     (b) stock transfer agent

     (c) minute book

33. (a) For the Year Ended

     (b) Prior period adjustment

     (c) Balance as restated

     (d) Net income, 19D

     (e) Dividends declared in 19D

     (f) Preferred stock

     (g) Stock; $5,000

     (h) Retained earnings balance, December 31, 19D, $145,000

34.

(1) I	(7) C	(13) E	(19) S	(25) U
(2) T	(8) AA	(14) Q	(20) X	(26) R
(3) W	(9) V	(15) A	(21) H	(27) BB
(4) N	(10) G	(16) Y	(22) J	(28) B
(5) F	(11) K	(17) L	(23) M	
(6) P	(12) Z	(18) O	(24) D	

Chapter 13

1. voting common stock; a debt security (e.g., a bond)

2. cost

3. F, the recorded cost does not include accrued interest.

4. (a) B; (b) C; (c) A

5. (a) C; (b) B; (c) A

6. (a) the ability to affect, in an important degree, the operating and financial policies of the other company. Usually 20 percent, but not more than 50 percent, of the outstanding common stock (i.e., the voting stock).
    (b) the ability to determine the operating and financial policies of the other company. Usually over 50 percent of the outstanding common stock (i.e., the voting stock).

7. (a) cost
   (b) equity
   (c) consolidated statement

8. D

9. B

10. *Case A*—Cost method must be used (10% ownership):

    (a) Long-term investments, common stock, Corporation B...... 75,000
        Cash 75,000

    (b) No entry under the cost method required for reported earnings of Corporation B.

    (c) Cash ($10,000 × 10%) 1,000
        Revenue from investments............................. 1,000

    (d) Unrealized loss on long-term investments
        (3,000 shares × $1) 3,000
        Allowance to reduce long-term investments to LCM 3,000

    Case B—Equity method must be used (30% ownership):

    (a) Long-term investments, common stock, Corporation B...... 225,000
        Cash 225,000

    (b) Long-term investments, common stock, Corporation B...... 6,000
        Revenue from investments ($20,000 × 30%).............. 6,000

    (c) Cash ($10,000 × 30%) 3,000
        Long-term investments, common stock, Corporation B.... 3,000

    (d) No entry for market under the equity method.

242

11. T

12. T

13. (a)
    B, $79,000, aggregate market because it is less than cost of $85,000
    (b) C, zero, the unrealized loss amount ($6,000) should be reported as a negative or contra amount on the 19B balance sheet
    (c) D
    (d) C

14. T

15. F, income is recorded when the investee company reports its net income.

16. (a) interest each period
    (b) principal at the maturity date

17. F, only common stock confers voting privileges.

18. (a), (b), and (c), the same: $1,000 × 5% = $50

19. T

20. $10,000 × 9% × 4/12 = $300

21. (a) $5,000 × 1.04 = $5,200

    (b) $5,200 − ($200 ÷ 4 years = $50) = $5,150

    (c) $5,200 − $200 = $5,000

22. T

23. (a) $1,070

    (b) $1,000 × 10% = $100

    (c) $1,070 − [($100 × 7 yrs. = $700) + $1,000] = $630

    (d) ($1,000 × 10% = $100) − ($70 ÷ 7 yrs. = $10) = $90 (or $630 ÷ 7 yrs. = $90)

24. Long-term investment, bonds 3,000
    Interest revenue ($3,000 × 10% × 2/12) 50
      Cash 3,050

25. Long-term investment, bonds 2,040
    Interest revenue ($2,000 × 9% × 2/12) 30
      Cash 2,070

26. Cash 1,000
    Loss on sale of long-term investment 20
      Bond investment ($1,050 − $30 amortization) 1,020

27. (1) D   (3) G   (5) F   (7) C
    (2) A   (4) B   (6) E

Chapter 14

1. F, an exception may occur with certain foreign subsidiaries

2. F, only the parent company prepares consolidated statements.

3. T

4. F, only the reporting of the parent is affected.

5. (a) more than 50 percent
   (b) parent and subsidiary

6. the separate financial statements of each are combined into one set of consolidated financial statements by the parent company.

7. control is evidenced by ownership of more than 50 percent of the outstanding voting stock of the other company

8. reporting

9. T

10. (a) pooling of interests
    (b) purchase

11. F, only in a purchase.

12. pooling of interests

13. book

14. (1) A; (2) B; (3) C

15. T

16. intercompany debt

17. (a) Purchase:

Investment in Company S stock	300,000	
Cash (10,000 shares × $30)......................		300,000

    (b) Pooling of interests:

Investment in Company S stock	240,000	
Common stock (20,000 shares × $5)		100,000
Contributed capital from pooling		140,000

18. market; book

19. F, pooling uses book value of the subsidiary whereas purchase uses market value.

20. as a combined entity there is no debt or receivable involving outsiders in such instances. If they are not eliminated, both debt to, and receivables from, within the entity would be overstated.

21. (a) purchase
    (b) pooling of interests

22.

	Pooling—Share for Share		Purchase	
Investment in Company S stock	170,000		192,000	
Common stock (12,000 shares × $2)		24,000		
Cash (12,000 shares × $16)				192,000
Contributed capital from pooling		146,000		

23. T

24. T

25. Goodwill computed:

Purchase price		$59,000
Net assets purchased (at market value):		
Assets	$64,000	
Less: Liabilities assumed	20,000	
Total market value purchased		44,000
Goodwill purchased		$15,000

26.

Combination by Purchase

		Eliminations		Balance Sheet
Assets:				
Cash				$ 19,000
Receivable from Company B	(b)	−$	4,000	
Inventories	(a)	−	2,000	54,000
Investment in Company B	(a)	−	38,000	
Equipment (net)	(a)	+	7,000	43,000
Goodwill	(a)	+	8,000*	8,000
Total				$124,000
Liabilities:				
Accounts payable				$ 14,000
Payable to Company A	(b)	−	4,000	
Stockholders' equity:				
Common stock:				
Company A (par $10)				80,000
Company B (par $5)	(a)	−	15,000	
Retained earnings:				
Company A				30,000
Company B	(a)	−	10,000	
Total				$124,000

*Computation of goodwill:		
Purchase price		$38,000
Net assets purchased (at market value):		
Cash	$ 9,000	
Inventory	14,000	
Equipment	13,000	
Less: Liabilities assumed	(6,000)	
Total market value purchased		30,000
Goodwill purchased		$ 8,000

27. (1) E   (3) G   (5) C   (7) B
     (2) A   (4) H   (6) D   (8) F

Chapter 15

1. (a) operating activities

   (b) investing activities

   (c) financing activities

2. earning net income

3. T

4. F, it is a cash flow from operating activities.

5. F, it is a cash flow from operating activities.

6. T

7. F, it is a cash flow from operating activities.

8. Short-term highly liquid investments

   (a) readily convertible to known amounts of cash.

   (b) so near their maturity that they present insignificant risk of changes in value because of changes in interest rates.

9. F, the net cash flow from operating activities is the same under the direct and indirect method.

10. direct

11. indirect

12. F, it cannot be prepared from a trial balance.

13. schedule approach

    spreadsheet approach

14. Noncash investing and financing activities

15. The activity that caused the gain or loss

16. (a) + decrease in

    (b) − increase in

17. (a) + decrease in

    (b) − increase in

18. $18,900

19. (a) −   (b) +
20. (a) +   (b) −
21. (a) +   (b) −
22. (a) −   (b) +
23. (a) −   (b) +

24. F, these activities are reported in a schedule or disclosure note.

25. F, it is added under the indirect method.

26. T

27. T

28. T

29.

(1)	G	(6)	C	(11)	J
(2)	K	(7)	D		
(3)	H	(8)	F		
(4)	A	(9)	B		
(5)	I	(10)	E		

Chapter 16

1. (a) Information about past performance of the enterprise
   (b) Information about the present condition of the enterprise
   (c) Information about the future performance (e.g., cash flows) of the enterprise.

2.

Income Statement	Component Percentages	Balance Sheet (Partial)	Component Percentages
Sales revenue	100%	Cash........................	24%
Expenses:		Operational assets	86
Cost of goods sold	(50)	Accumulated depreciation	(25)
Remaining expenses	(40)	Patent	10
Net income................	10	Other assets	5
		Total assets	100

3.

	Amount	Percent
Income statement:		
Sales revenue	$3,000	5%
Expenses	(500)	(1)
Net income	$3,500	35
Balance sheet:		
Liabilities...........	$(3,000)	(30)
Common stock	20,000	20
Retained earnings ...	(10,000)	(25)
Total.............	$7,000	5

4. profitability

5. market

6. liquidity

7. (a) income; (b) investment

8. resources used to earn the net income

9. (a) current (working capital) (b) quick

10. receivable turnover

11. inventory turnover (or average days of supply of inventory)

12. debt/equity ratio

13. financial leverage

14. (a) Dividends per share ÷ market price per share
    (b) Market price per share ÷ EPS

15. F, a very high inventory turnover, for example, may indicate that the company frequently is "out of stock."

16.

		Computations	Answer
	(1)	$10,000 ÷ $130,000 =	7.7%
	(2)	($10,000 + $600) ÷ $200,000 =	5.3%
	(3)	7.7% − 5.3% =	2.4%
	(4)	$10,000 ÷ 1,000 shares =	$10
	(5)	$10,000 ÷ $100,000 =	10.0%
	(6)	$30,000 ÷ $20,000 =	1.5 to 1
	(7)	$15,000 ÷ $20,000 =	0.75 to 1
	(8)	$40,000 ÷ $\frac{(\$14,000 + \$10,000)}{2}$ =	3.3 times
	(9)	$60,000 ÷ $\frac{(\$11,000 + \$15,000)}{2}$ =	4.6 times
	(10)	$70,000 ÷ $130,000 =	0.54
	(11)	$130,000 ÷ $200,000 =	0.65
	(12)	$70,000 ÷ $200,000 =	0.35
	(13)	$65 ÷ $10 =	6.5
	(14)	$2.60 ÷ $65 =	4.0%
	(15)	($100,000 + $30,000) ÷ ($100,000 ÷ $100)	$130

17.

(a)	D		(f)	C
(b)	G		(g)	I
(c)	E		(h)	F
(d)	H		(i)	A
(e)	B		(j)	J

18.

(1)	E		(5)	G
(2)	C		(6)	H
(3)	F		(7)	D
(4)	A		(8)	B